science for a changing world

Prepared in cooperation with the U.S. Forest Service

# Connecticut Highlands Technical Report – *Documentation of the Regional Rainfall-Runoff Model*

Open-File Report 2010–1187

**U.S. Department of the Interior**
**U.S. Geological Survey**

1

Prepared in cooperation with the U.S. Forest Service

# Connecticut Highlands Technical Report – *Documentation of the Regional Rainfall-Runoff Model*

By Elizabeth A. Ahearn and David M. Bjerklie

Open-File Report 2010–1187

U.S. Department of the Interior
U.S. Geological Survey

**U.S. Department of the Interior**
KEN SALAZAR, Secretary

**U.S. Geological Survey**
Marcia K. McNutt, Director

U.S. Geological Survey, Reston, Virginia:  2010

For product and ordering information:
World Wide Web: http://www.usgs.gov/pubprod
Telephone: 1-888-ASK-USGS

For more information on the USGS—the Federal source for science about the Earth,
its natural and living resources, natural hazards, and the environment:
World Wide Web:  http://www.usgs.gov
Telephone:  1-888-ASK-USGS

# Contents

# Figures

## Tables

# Connecticut Highlands Technical Report – *Documentation of the Regional Rainfall-Runoff Model*

## SECTION 1. WATER RESOURCES

### Purpose and Scope

This report provides the supporting data and describes the data sources, methodologies, and assumptions used in the assessment of existing and potential water resources of the Highlands of Connecticut and Pennsylvania (referred to herein as the "Highlands"). Included in this report are Highlands groundwater and surface-water use data nd the methods of data compilation. Annual mean streamflow and annual mean base-flow estimates from selected U.S. Geological Survey (USGS) gaging stations were computed using data for the period of record through water year 2005. The methods of watershed modeling are discussed and regional and sub-regional water budgets are provided. Information on Highlands surface-water-quality trends is presented. USGS web sites are provided as sources for additional information on groundwater levels, streamflow records, and ground- and surface-water-quality data. Interpretation of these data and the findings are summarized in the Highlands study report (Connecticut–Pennsylvania Highlands Regional Study, written commun., E.A. Ahearn, 2008).

### 1.1. Groundwater – Aquifers and Community Wells

Groundwater systems store and transmit water and enable communities and individual well owners to obtain water without constructing pipelines or storage facilities. From a regional perspective, the groundwater resource appears ample. Throughout the Highlands, however, the availability of groundwater varies widely. Understanding the limits of the aquifers (groundwater sources of water) is a key aspect of a groundwater assessment.

A total of 196 community wells are in the Highlands study area. Community wells are defined as public drinking-water systems that serve at least 25 residents throughout the year. The locations these wells with safe yields of more than 0.001 million gallons per day (Mgal/d) operating in 2000, and information on the type of aquifer are shown in figure 1 and listed in Appendix 1, CT_community_wells. To describe and assess the groundwater resource, information on the hydrogeology of the aquifers and information about groundwater use (safe yield and demand) were compiled. An aquifer is defined as any geological formation such as sand, soil, gravel, or porous rock that can store and supply ground water to wells and springs. High-yielding aquifers composed of coarse-grained stratified sediment such as sand and gravel are limited in areal extent. Low-yielding till aquifers cover most of the Highlands area. The term "safe yield" is defined as the maximum dependable quantity of water per unit of time that may flow or be pumped continuously from a source of supply during a critical dry period without consideration of available water limitations. (State of Connecticut, 2008). Groundwater safe yields—as opposed to well yields—were compiled for community wells used for municipal supply, industrial, commercial, irrigation, and mining uses. Generally, well yield is the withdrawal rate of water from the well (groundwater system) and is a function of the pump capacity.

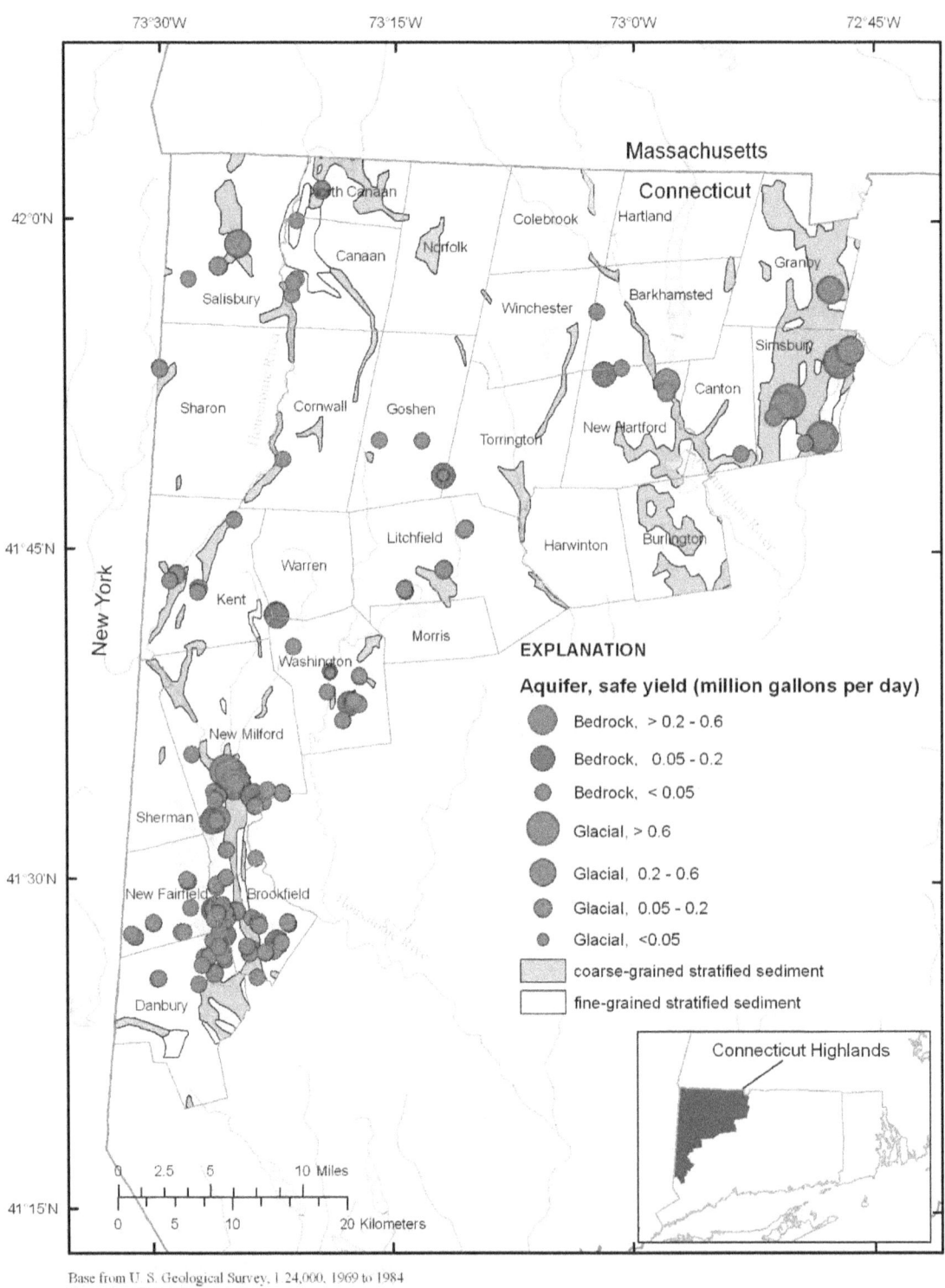

**Figure 1.** Location of 196 community wells with safe yields of more than 0.001 Mgal/d operating in 2000 in the Highlands study area. Areas not shown as underlain by stratified sediment are underlain by till.

Well yields for community wells are not readily available, and therefore, information on safe yields was used to estimate annual groundwater withdrawals from the community wells. In general, these withdrawals are about 75 percent of the total safe yield. During summer, groundwater withdrawals from the smaller community systems can reach 90 to 100 percent of their safe yields (Steve Messer, Connecticut Department of Public Health, oral commun., May 9, 2008).

Forty-six of the 196 community wells are in stratified glacial deposits. The safe yields of wells in stratified glacial deposits ranged from 0.06 to 1.14 Mgal/d; the combined safe yield in 2000 was 15.3 Mgal/d (Connecticut Department of Public Health, Water Supply Division, community well database, written commun., 2001). A total of 150 of the 196 wells are in bedrock (both crystalline and carbonate). The safe yields of most wells in bedrock ranged from 0.001 to 0.162 Mgal/d; however, one bedrock well had a reported safe yield of 0.43 Mgal/d. Although there are substantially more wells in bedrock than in stratified glacial deposits in the study area, the combined safe yield of wells in bedrock was 3.92 Mgal/d in 2000, considerably less than the combined safe yield of wells in stratified glacial deposits. The annual groundwater withdrawals from the community wells in the Highlands were estimated to be about 14.4 Mgal/d (assumed as 75 percent of the total safe yield).

## 1.2. Groundwater-Level Data

Groundwater levels from selected USGS network observation wells (fig. 2) provide information on how water levels within the Highlands aquifers respond to seasonal changes in climate, changes in recharge patterns, and groundwater withdrawals. Groundwater levels typically are highest in winter and early spring because of reduced evapotranspiration, low temperatures, snowmelt, and spring rains that recharge the aquifers. Typically groundwater levels start to decline as summer begins and continue to decline through late fall because more water evaporates from the land surface and transpires from plants reducing recharge. Groundwater levels are typically lowest in late fall. A list of the USGS groundwater observation wells within the Highlands study area is presented in table 1. The locations of the groundwater observation wells are shown in figure 2. Each observation well is identified by (1) a 15-digit number based on latitude and longitude (USGS groundwater well ID) and (2) a local number based on a town code and a sequential number (Local ID). Typically, water-level measurements are made monthly in these wells.

**Table 1.** U.S. Geological Survey groundwater observation wells, Highlands study area, 2005.

| USGS Groundwater Well ID | Local ID | Town | Years of record | Well depth from land surface (feet) | Aquifer |
|---|---|---|---|---|---|
| 413007073250501 | BD8 | Brookfield | 40 | 53.0 | glacial, sand & gravel |
| 414649072574401 | BU144 | Burlington | 10 | 13.1 | glacial, sand & gravel |
| 414704072580501 | BU143 | Burlington | 10 | 21.3 | glacial, sand & gravel |
| 414615072581601 | BU2 | Burlington | 50 | 42.7 | unknown |
| 415649072494801 | GR328 | Granby | 25 | 22.0 | glacial, till |
| 415643072502201 | GR330 | Granby | 24 | 22.0 | glacial, sand & gravel |
| 415647072495901 | GR329 | Granby | 24 | 22.0 | glacial, till |
| 415653072501701 | GR331 | Granby | 23 | 31.5 | glacial, sand & gravel |
| 420125073193001 | NOC7 | North Canaan | 48 | 12.0 | glacial, sand & gravel |
| 415925073252001 | SY15 | Salisbury | 40 | 27.4 | glacial, stratified drift |
| 415956073241501 | SY24 | Salisbury | 20 | 28.7 | glacial, stratified drift |
| 415559073253401 | SY23 | Salisbury | 19 | 51.0 | glacial, till |

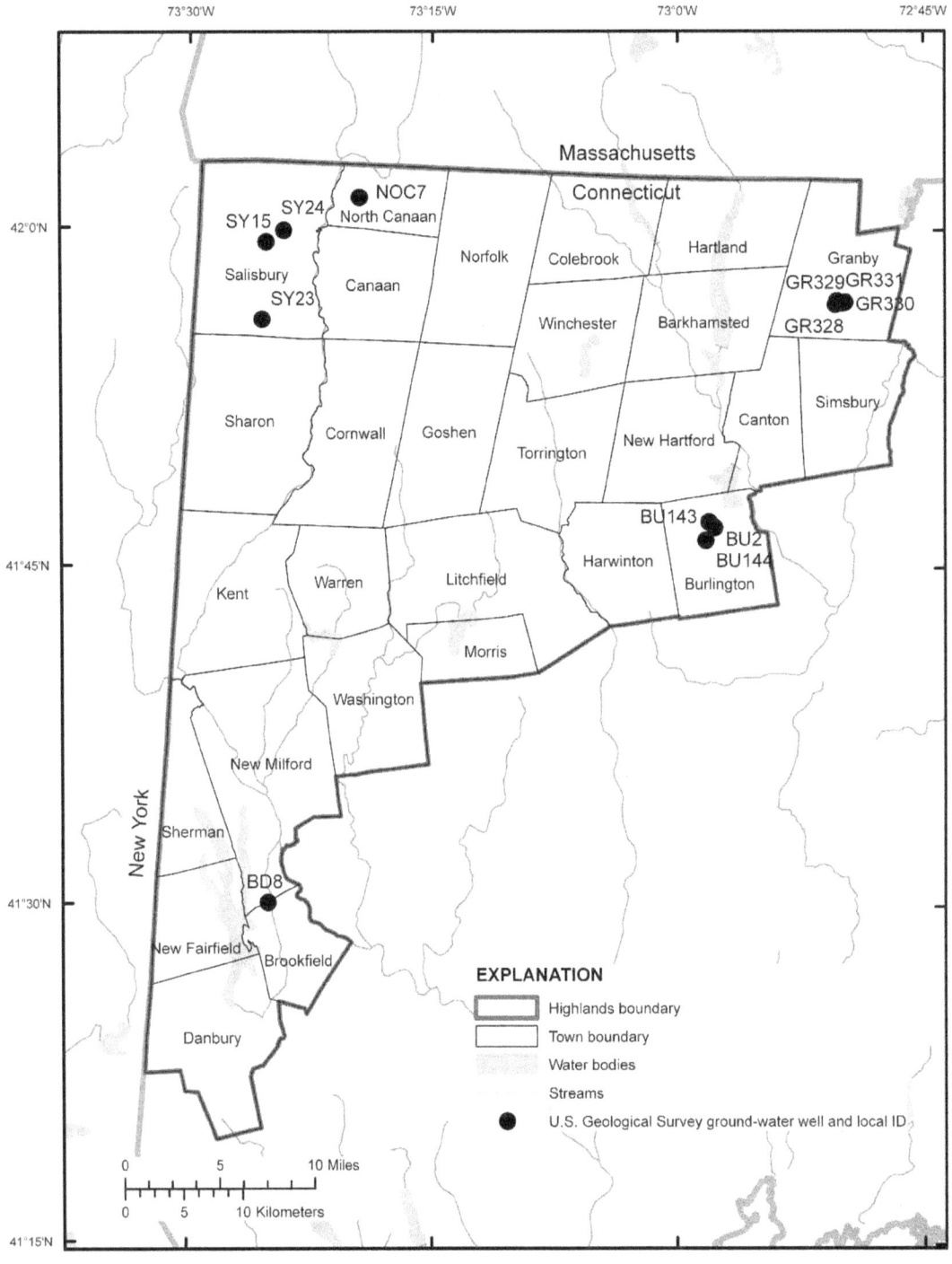

**Figure 2.** Location of U.S. Geological Survey groundwater wells in the Highlands study area.

Groundwater-level data collected by the USGS, associated well information, water-level hydrographs, and site maps can be accessed from the USGS National Water Information System, (NWIS), (U.S. Geological Survey, 2008a) (fig. 3).

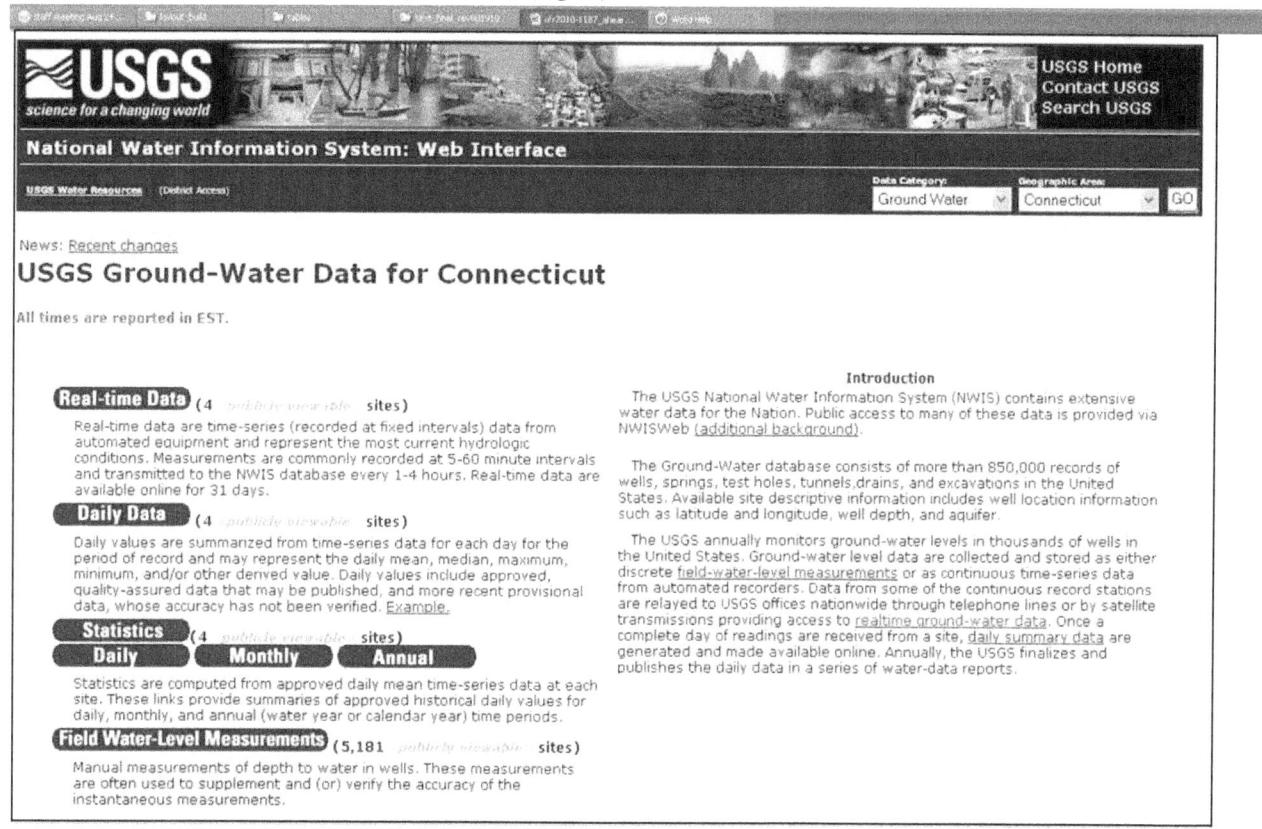

**Figure 3.**  Groundwater data for Connecticut (web site) (U.S. Geological Survey, 2008).

## 1.3. Surface Water - Streamflow Data and Base-Flow Estimates from Streamflow Records

Systematic records on daily streamflow are fundamental to streamflow analyses and forecasting water availability at national, regional, and local scales. Streamflow records for 37 streamflow-gaging stations in the Highlands study were retrieved from the USGS NWIS. The 37 stations have drainage areas ranging from 3 to 996 square miles ($mi^2$); the median drainage area is 38 $mi^2$. Each of the stations had 5 or more years of daily streamflow record through September 2005. A list of streamflow-gaging stations in the Highlands study area including information on the station latitude, longitude, town location, years of record, period of record (month and years of operation), and drainage area (area of watershed above the stream gage) is provided in table 2. The locations of streamflow-gaging stations are shown in figure 4.

The highest and lowest annual mean streamflow for the period of record and the mean annual streamflow at each gaging station are provided in Appendix 1, CT_streamflow. The highest and lowest annual mean streamflows for the period of record were obtained by ranking the individual annual-mean streamflows. The mean annual streamflow was obtained by dividing the sum of all the individual (water year) annual mean flows by the number of water years. Mean annual streamflow in

**Table 2.** List of USGS streamflow-gaging stations in the Highlands study area including information on the station's latitude, longitude, town location, year of record, period of record, and drainage area.

[ID, identification number; USGS, U.S. Geological Survey; mi², square miles; bold italic type indicates station with no or minimum flow alteration.]

| Map ID (from fig. 4) | USGS station number | Latitude (decimal degrees) | Longitude (decimal degrees) | River name | Town | Years of record | Period of record | Drainage area (mi²) |
|---|---|---|---|---|---|---|---|---|
| 1 | 01186000 | 41.9629 | -73.0176 | West Branch Farmington River | Barkhamsted | 50 | Oct 1955 - Sep 2005 | 131 |
| 2 | 01186100 | 41.9309 | -73.0818 | Mad River | Winchester | 13 | Oct 1956 - Sep 1969 | 18.5 |
| 3 | 01186400 | 41.9783 | -73.0456 | Sandy Brook | Colebrook | 9 | Oct 1967 - Sep 1976 | 34.9 |
| 4 | 01186500 | 41.9673 | -73.0340 | Still River | Colebrook | 55 | Oct 1948 - Jul 1967, Jul 1969 -Sep 2005 | 85.0 |
| 5 | 01187000 | 41.9537 | -73.0137 | West Branch Farmington River | Barkhamsted | 26 | Oct 1929 - Sep 1955 | 217 |
| 6 | *01187300* | *42.0373* | *-72.9390* | *Hubbard River* | *Hartland* | *66* | *Jan 1938 - Sep 1955, Oct 1956 - Sep 2005* | *19.9* |
| 7 | *01187400* | *42.0343* | *-72.9298* | *Valley Brook* | *Hartland* | *32* | *Oct 1940 - Sep 1972* | *7.03* |
| 8 | *01187680* | *41.8723* | *-72.9062* | *Cherry Brook* | *Canton* | *5* | *Oct 1966 - Sep 1971* | *8.23* |
| 9 | *01187800* | *41.8207* | *-72.9701* | *Nepaug River* | *New Hartford* | *52* | *Oct 1921 - Sep 1955, Oct 1957 - Sep 1972, Oct 1998 - Sep 2001* | *23.5* |
| 10 | 01187980 | 41.7993 | -72.9254 | Farmington River | Avon | 15 | Nov 1962 - Sep 1977 | 360 |
| 11 | *01188000* | *41.7862* | *-72.9648* | *Burlington Brook* | *Burlington* | *74* | *Oct 1931 - Sep 2005* | *4.10* |
| 12 | 01188090 | 41.7559 | -72.8868 | Farmington River | Farmington | 28 | Oct 1977 - Sep 2005 | 378 |
| 13 | 01189000 | 41.6732 | -72.9007 | Pequabuck River | Bristol | 64 | Oct 1941 - Sep 2005 | 45.8 |
| 14 | 01189200 | 41.8701 | -72.8243 | Stratton Brook | Simsbury | 5 | Oct 1966 - Sep 1971 | 5.13 |
| 15 | 01189210 | 41.8732 | -72.8234 | Hop Brook | Simsbury | 5 | Oct 1966 - Sep 1971 | 10.7 |
| 16 | 01189390 | 41.9543 | -72.7795 | East Branch Salmon Brook | Granby | 13 | Oct 1963 - Oct 1976 | 39.5 |
| 17 | 01189500 | 41.9373 | -72.7762 | Salmon Brook | East Granby | 17 | Oct 1946 - Sep 1963 | 67.4 |
| 18 | 01189995 | 41.9084 | -72.7607 | Farmington River | Simsbury | 34 | Oct 1971 - Sep 2005 | 577 |
| 19 | 01198500 | 42.0240 | -73.3418 | Blackberry River | North Canaan | 22 | Oct 1949 - Oct 1971 | 45.9 |
| 20 | 01199000 | 41.9573 | -73.3693 | Housatonic River | Salisbury | 93 | Oct 1912 - Sep 2005 | 634 |
| 21 | 01199050 | 41.9423 | -73.3910 | Salmon Creek | Salisbury | 44 | Oct 1961 - Sep 2005 | 29.4 |
| 22 | *01199200* | *41.8243* | *-73.4301* | *Guinea Brook* | *Sharon* | *21* | *Aug 1960 - Oct 1981* | *3.50* |
| 23 | 01199290 | 41.7267 | -73.4819 | Housatonic River | Kent | 4 | May 1985 - Dec 1989 | 756 |
| 24 | 01200000 | 41.6589 | -73.5289 | Tenmile River | Wingdale, NY | 73 | Oct 1929 - Sep 1987, Oct 1991 - Sep 2005 | 203 |
| 25 | 01200500 | 41.6531 | -73.4898 | Housatonic River | New Milford | 65 | Oct 1940 - Sep 2005 | 996 |
| 26 | *01201190* | *41.6079* | *-73.4246* | *West Aspetuck River* | *New Milford* | *10* | *Oct 1962 - Sep 1972* | *23.8* |
| 27 | 01201500 | 41.5201 | -73.4182 | Still River | New Milford | 35 | Oct 1931 - Sep 1966 | 67.5 |
| 28 | 01201510 | 41.5367 | -73.4178 | Still River | New Milford | 5 | Oct 1966 - Sep 1971 | 69.6 |
| 29 | *01201930* | *41.7895* | *-73.2590* | *Marshepaug River* | *Goshen* | *14* | *Oct 1967 - Oct 1981* | *9.24* |
| 30 | 01202500 | 41.7233 | -73.2936 | Shepaug River | Litchfield | 6 | Oct 1960 - Sep 1966 | 38.0 |
| 31 | 01202501 | 41.7192 | -73.2933 | Shepaug River | Litchfield | 5 | Oct 2000 - Sep 2005 | 38.1 |
| 32 | 01203000 | 41.5497 | -73.3303 | Shepaug River | Roxbury | 46 | Oct 1930 - Sep 1971 Mar 2001 - Sep 2005 | 132 |
| 33 | 01205600 | 41.8009 | -73.1234 | W Brook Naugatuck River | Torrington | 40 | Oct 1956 - Sep 1992, Oct 1993 - Apr 1997 | 33.8 |
| 34 | 01205700 | 41.8034 | -73.1179 | East Branch Naugatuck River | Torrington | 41 | Oct 1956 - Apr 1997 | 13.6 |
| 35 | 01206000 | 41.7043 | -73.0643 | Naugatuck River | Thomaston | 29 | Oct 1930 - Sep 1959 | 71.0 |
| 36 | *01206400* | *41.7295* | *-73.0532* | *Leadmine Brook* | *Harwinton* | *13* | *Oct 1960 - Oct 1973* | *19.6* |
| 37 | *01206500* | *41.7018* | *-73.0573* | *Leadmine Brook* | *Thomaston* | *29* | *Oct 1930 - Sep 1959* | *24.3* |

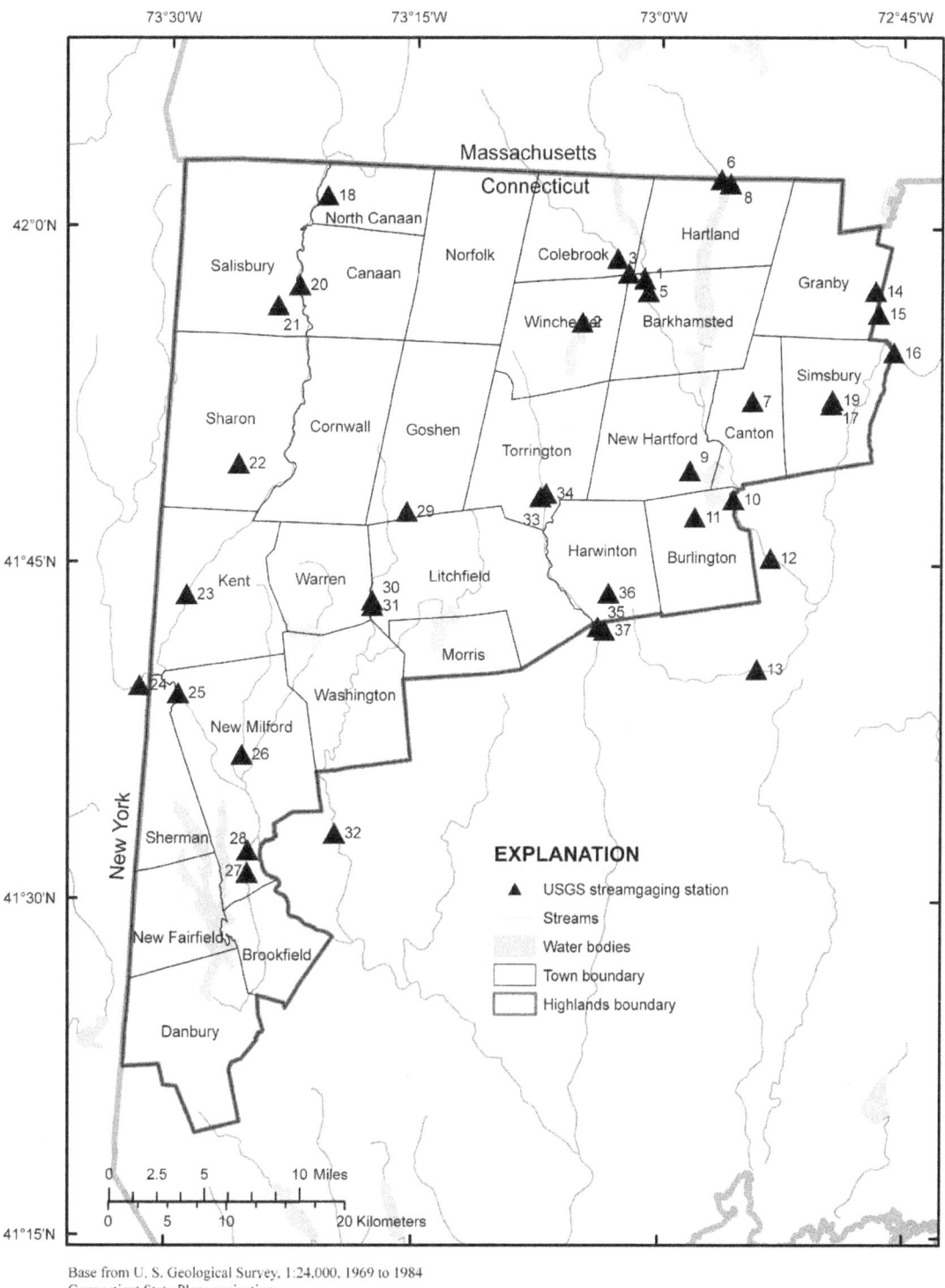

Base from U. S. Geological Survey. 1:24,000, 1969 to 1984
Connecticut State Plane projection

**Figure 4.** Location of U.S. Geological Survey streamflow-gaging stations in the Highlands study area with 5 or more years of continuous record through September 2005.

13

cubic feet per second per square mile and mean annual streamflow in inches over the drainage basin also are included. These values allow planners and researchers to compare the hydrologic characteristics of watersheds regardless of differences in their size. Mean annual streamflow in cubic feet per second per square mile is the annual average of the cubic feet of water flowing per second past a gaging station for each square mile of area drained above the station, and assumes runoff to be distributed uniformly in time and area. Mean annual streamflow in inches over the drainage basin is the depth to which the drainage area would be covered if all the annual streamflow were uniformly distributed over it. The mean annual streamflow in inches is commonly compared to mean annual precipitation. On an average annual basis, the Highlands receives about 49 in. of precipitation. The mean annual streamflow in inches over the drainage basin can be thought of as the amount of water that enters the basin as precipitation and leaves the basin as streamflow, after being diminished by evapotranspiration and ground- or surface-water withdrawals. The mean annual streamflow over the Highlands study area is about 25 in.

## Base-Flow Estimates from Streamflow Records

Total streamflow can be separated into two components—runoff and base flow. Runoff consists of overland runoff, interflow (water that travels laterally within the unsaturated zone during or directly after a precipitation event and discharges to streams without recharging the water table), and precipitation that falls directly on surface-water bodies. Base flow is composed of groundwater discharge. The amount of base flow in a stream is a measure of the infiltration capacity and yield of the underlying groundwater system. Base-flow conditions within a watershed can be equated to the amount of groundwater recharge in the watershed when averaged over the long term. Runoff and base flow are two important components of the water-budget analysis. Changes in runoff or base flow are strong indicators of changes in watershed conditions.

Hydrograph separation techniques are used to separate surface (runoff) and groundwater flows (base flow). Most hydrograph-separation techniques identify times of negligible runoff where base flow (groundwater discharge) equals streamflow; base flow is then interpolated between these periods. The automated hydrograph-separation technique called PART used in this report and described by Rutledge (1998) uses streamflow partitioning to separate the runoff and groundwater components of streamflow. The principal assumption of this method is that base flow is equal to streamflow on days that fit a requirement of antecedent recession; that is, streamflow on any one day is greater than or equal to streamflow on the following day with a subsequent decline of not more than one-tenth of a logarithmic cycle. When days do not fit this requirement, the larger declines or increased streamflow are assumed to result from changes in the runoff portion of streamflow, and the groundwater portion of streamflow is determined by linear interpolation.

The automated hydrograph-separation technique–PART (Rutledge, 1998)–was used to estimate annual mean base flow for each water year at 36 of 37 gaging stations in the Highlands study area. The hydrograph-separation technique was not applied to one station (Housatonic River at Gaylordsville, USGS 01200500) because of the known large extent of flow alteration. The hydrograph-separation technique is intended for analyzing a groundwater-flow system that is considered natural, with negligible anthropogenic effects to the hydrologic flow regime. Only 28 percent of the stations (10 of 36) have natural streamflow (no water withdrawals or point-source releases in the drainage area above the gaging station); this data set is not large enough to characterize base-flow conditions throughout the Highlands. Subsequently, the hydrograph-separation technique was used to estimate annual mean base flows at the remaining 72 percent of the stations (26 of 36) in the Highlands region, many of which are affected by water withdrawals, streamflow diversions, regulation, point-source discharges, and (or)

14

reservoir operations. The results from the hydrograph-separation technique from the altered basins help determine if streamflow will be sufficient for water-quality and aquatic-habitat needs.

Mean annual base-flow estimates for the 36 stations described above are provided in Appendix 1, CT_streamflow. Mean annual base flow was obtained by dividing the sum of all the individual annual base flows by the number of recorded water years for each gaging station. Calculated base flow ranged from about 58 to 86 percent of streamflow; the average was 70 percent for the 36 stations. For the 10 basins with natural flow, base flows ranged from 58 to 78 percent of streamflow. For the 26 basins with altered flows, base flows are slightly higher than the basins with natural flows, ranging from 62 to 86 percent of streamflow. To some extent, the higher base-flow estimates from the PART program may be explained by regulated releases that artificially increase base flow; the PART program interprets most regulated releases as base flow.

In Connecticut, the highest base-flow percentages and continuous groundwater discharges to streams during dry weather and droughts generally are associated with those basins underlain with a high percentage of thick deposits of stratified glacial deposits. Not all the basins with natural flow in the Highlands appear to follow this pattern. With only 10 stations in the data set, the range of each geologic characteristic is very limited. For example, only Bunnell (Burlington) Brook has more than 7 percent stratified glacial deposits. Although the percentage of base flow calculated by the PART program at this site is not the highest value for the 10 stations analyzed, the stream has never been dry. Another explanation for why some of the streams in the Highlands with low percentages of stratified glacial deposits have some of the highest base flow in the region could be that most of these basins are very small and the groundwater drainage area may not coincide with the surface-water drainage area (defined by the topographic drainage divide). Therefore, base flow may be sustained by ground water from aquifer areas outside the topographic drainage divide. Lower base-flow percentages generally are associated with basins containing high percentages of impervious cover or water withdrawals.

For basins with altered flows, the highest base-flow percentages generally are associated with those basins that have point-source discharges (e.g., wastewater releases from sewage-treatment facilities or industries), are underlain with a high percentage of thick deposits of glacial deposits, and are waste-receiving streams.

## Additional Streamflow Data

Detailed records of stream stage, discharge, streamflow statistics, peak discharge, long-term streamflow hydrographs, and descriptive surface-water site information for gaging stations in the Highlands or other areas of Connecticut can be accessed from the USGS NWIS (U.S. Geological Survey, 2008b) (fig. 5).

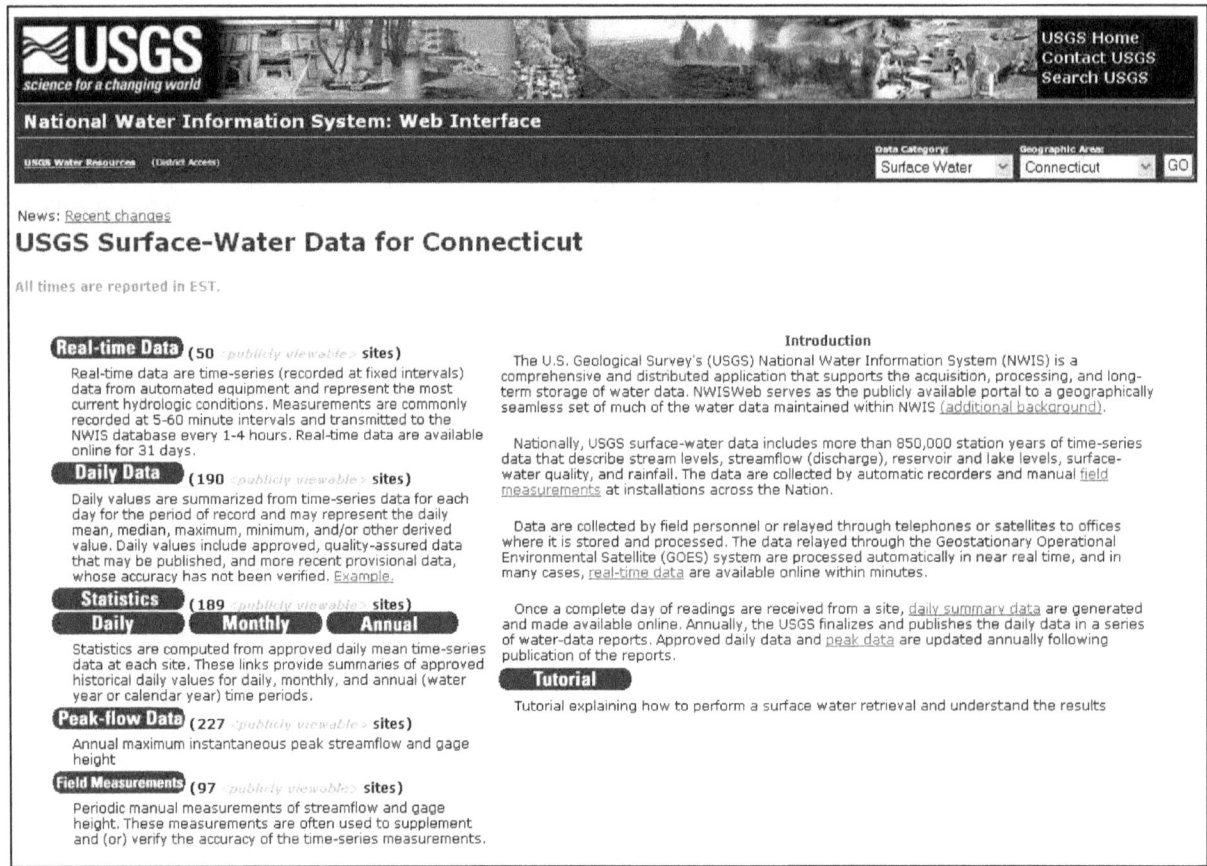

**Figure 5.** Surface-water data for Connecticut (web site) (U.S. Geological Survey, 2008).

## 1.4. Water Withdrawals and Water Use

In order to evaluate existing hydrologic conditions within the Highlands study area, an assessment of the volume of water withdrawn from aquifers and reservoirs was performed. Site-specific and aggregated data on withdrawals of ground water and surface water in 2005 were collected and compiled with other reported and estimated water-use data. In Connecticut, three state agencies—Department of Environmental Protection (DEP), Department of Public Health (DPH), and Department of Public Utility Control (DPUC)—are involved in the collection and compilation of water-use information.

The Connecticut DEP has the regulatory authority to allocate groundwater and surface-water resources through the Water Division Program. In Connecticut, a diversion permit is required for groundwater or surface-water withdrawals greater than or equal to 50,000 gallons per day (gal/d) on any given day. There are two types of water diversions – registered diversions ("grandfathered" diversions) and permitted diversions. The state has no regulatory control over registered diversions; it does have control over permitted diversions. Owners of permitted diversions are required to record water withdrawals daily and report total water withdrawals to DEP annually. Individuals with registered diversions are requested to maintain daily logs of their water use but are not required to report water withdrawals to any state agency (as of January 2008). In the Connecticut Highlands, there are 162 registered diversions and 67 permitted diversions (permitted diversions represent 127 diversion locations). Estimates of the registered and permitted water withdrawals in the Highlands can serve as an upper limit of water use and withdrawals. A list of the registered and permitted diversions is available through the Inland Water Resources Division of the Connecticut DEP (Connecticut Department of Environmental Protection, 2008).

The Connecticut DPH has regulatory oversight of the State's drinking-water systems for ensuring safety and adequacy of drinking-water supplies of community water systems. Water suppliers of community systems are required to report monthly to the DPH the quantity and quality of the water withdrawals. Information on community water-supply systems is available through the Drinking Water Section of the Connecticut DPH (Connecticut Department of Public Health, 2008a).

The Connecticut DPUC is charged by statute with the regulation of investor-owned water companies. The investor-owned water companies are required to report annually to the DPUC the quantities of water delivered to consumers, or lost or unaccounted for, and the system demand. Metered sales of water for residential, commercial, industrial, and public authorities are included in the annual reports to the DPUC by investor-owned water companies. Information on water production and consumption from investor-owned water companies, including quantities of water produced and delivered to consumers during the year, can be obtained from the DPUC (Connecticut Department of Public Utility Control, 2008).

## Estimating Domestic Water Use

Domestic water use was estimated for the 28 towns and cities in the Highlands primarily using population data and a per-capita water-use coefficient (Appendix 1, Domestic Use). Data on populations served by public supply were obtained from the Connecticut DPH Community Water System database (Connecticut Department of Public Health, 2008b). The number of self-supplied people was determined by subtracting the population served by community water systems (about 154,000) from the city or town populations (300,000 total) as reported by the U.S. Bureau of the Census (2005). The difference between the population served by community water systems and the total population indicated that 47 percent of the population (about 145,000) was self-supplied in 2005. A per-capita water-use coefficient, 85 gal/d per person, representing the average amount of water typically used for domestic purposes, was multiplied by the populations (self-supplied and public supplied for each town and city) to estimate domestic water use. All self-supplied domestic water use was assumed to be from ground water.

The self-supplied populations were cross-checked using information from 1990 U.S. Bureau of the Census data (1990), which reported about 60,000 private wells in the Highlands. The 1990 U.S. Census of Housing provides data on "source of water" (public system or private company, individual drilled well, or some other source) by housing unit, as well as the number of total housing units by municipality. Data on the number of individual wells and or households served by public systems were not compiled for the 2005 U.S. Census.

The per-capita water-use coefficient was obtained from a report by the USGS on water use (Solley, 1998). A detailed study in coastal Connecticut (Fairfield County) has shown per-capita water use can vary from as little as 50 to as much as 1,000 gal/d depending on lot size, housing type, household income, type of supply (community, dug well, drilled well), and water-use infrastructure (pools and landscape-irrigation systems) (Mullaney, 2004). The per-capita water-use coefficient used to estimate domestic water use in the Highlands, 85 gal/d per person, is slightly higher than the national average per-capita use coefficient, 80 gal/d per person (Solley, 1998).

## 1.5. Water Quality

The USGS monitors water-quality conditions in Connecticut and maintains a database of water-quality records on a number of different physical properties, chemical constituents, and bacteria. Ten surface-water-quality stations, part of a larger network of water-quality stations throughout Connecticut, are used to monitor and or assess water-quality conditions of Highlands streams and rivers. A list of the 10 USGS water-quality stations in or near the Highlands study area is presented in table 3. The locations of the 10 water-quality stations are shown in figure 6.

**Table 3.** U.S. Geological Survey water-quality stations with 5 or more years of record in or near the Highlands study area, 2005.

[mi$^2$, square miles]

| U.S. Geological Survey station number | Latitude (decimal degrees) | Longitude (decimal degrees) | River name | Town | Years of record | Period of record (Water Years[1]) | Drainage area (mi$^2$) |
|---|---|---|---|---|---|---|---|
| 01188000 | 41.7862 | 72.9648 | Burlington Brook | Burlington | 39 | 1956, 1968-2005 | 4.10 |
| 01188090 | 41.7559 | 72.8868 | Farmington River | Farmington | 26 | 1977-80, 1984-2005 | 378 |
| 01189030 | 41.7167 | 72.8403 | Pequabuck River | Bristol | 33 | 1971, 1974-2005 | 57.2 |
| 01189995 | 41.9084 | 72.7607 | Farmington River | Simsbury | 37 | 1967-68, 1971-2005 | 577 |
| 01198125 | 42.0747 | 73.3339 | Housatonic River | Ashley Falls, MA | 15 | 1991-2005 | 465 |
| 01198990 | 41.9625 | 73.3717 | Falls Village Reservoir | Salisbury | 50 | 1956-2005 | 633 |
| 01200600 | 41.5931 | 73.4500 | Housatonic River | New Milford | 31 | 1962, 1963, 1974-91, 1995-2005 | 1,022 |
| 01201487 | 41.4661 | 73.4036 | Still River | Brookfield | 22 | 1984-2005 | 62.3 |
| 01203000 | 41.5497 | 73.3303 | Shepaug River | Roxbury | 35 | 1953, 1954, 1959, 1974-2005 | 132 |
| 01208049 | 41.6153 | 73.0583 | Naugutuck River | Waterbury | 27 | 1967, 1980-2005 | 136 |

[1] A water year is the 12-month period October 1 through September 30. The water year is designated by the calendar year in which it ends.

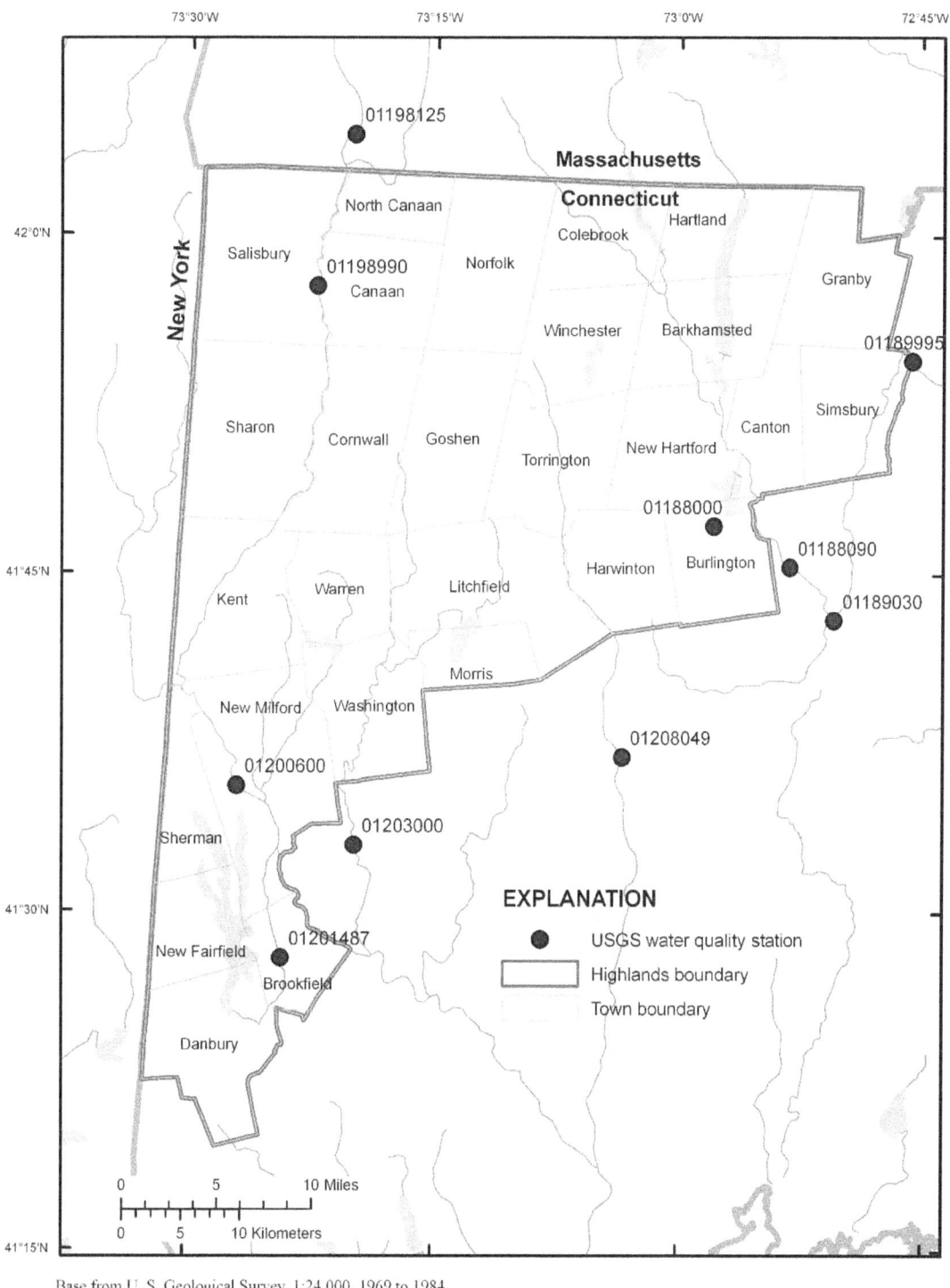

**Figure 6.**   Location of U.S. Geological Survey water-quality stations in the Highlands study area.

Water-quality data collected by the USGS can be retrieved through the USGS NWIS (U.S. Geological Survey, 2008c) (fig. 7).

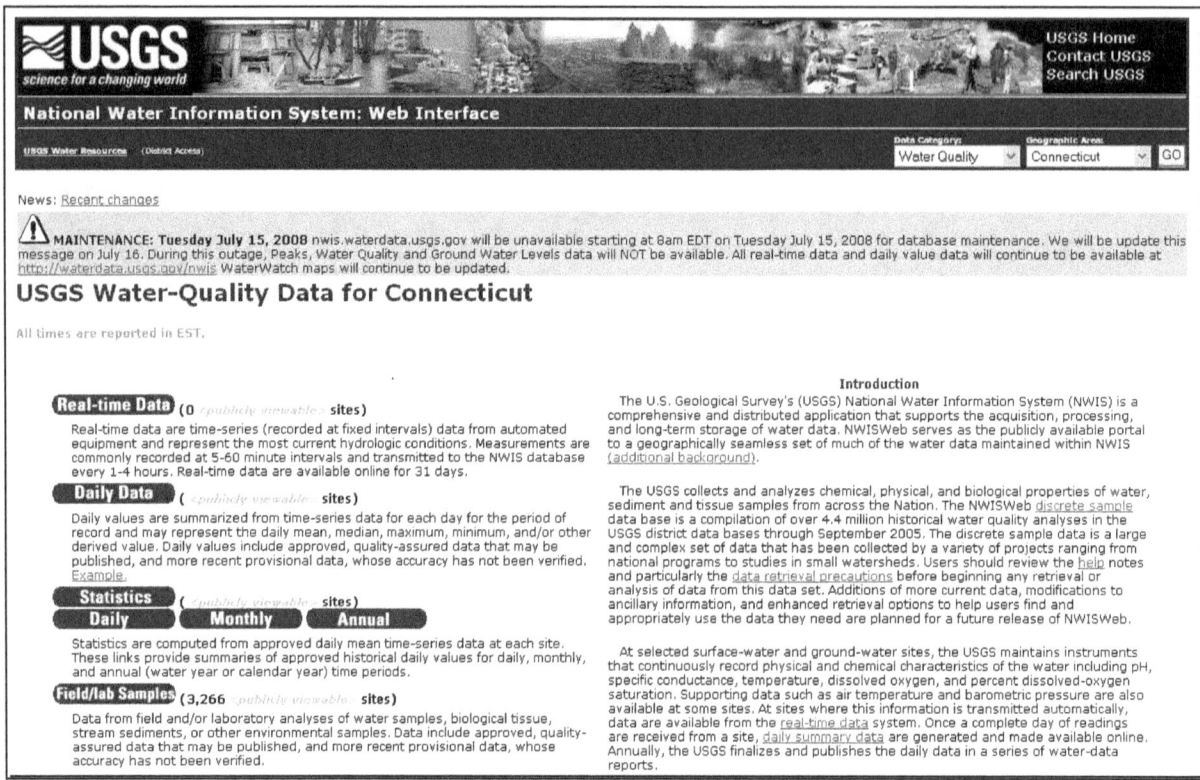

**Figure 7.**    Water-quality data for Connecticut (web site) (U.S. Geological Survey, 2008).

As part of the National Water-Quality Assessment (NAWQA) Program, the USGS began a study to identify, describe, and explain the natural and human factors that affect observed water-quality conditions and trends in some of the Nation's large river basins and aquifer systems. The Housatonic River Basin was included in this program. The primary objective of the study was to determine the occurrence and distribution of inorganic and organic water-quality constituents in shallow, recently recharged water beneath areas of undeveloped (forested), agricultural, and urban land use. The second objective was to relate variations in groundwater quality to natural and human factors.

The results of the NAWQA study in the Housatonic River Basin, including descriptions of the locations of the monitoring wells and water samples collected, are described by Grady and Mullaney (1998). The report indicates that 1) urbanization and agriculture have contributed to excess concentrations of nitrate nitrogen and the presence of volatile organic compounds and pesticides, 2) concentrations of nitrate nitrogen beneath urban and agricultural areas are frequently as much as 20 times higher than concentrations in forested areas, and 3) pesticides rarely exceed any established maximum contaminant levels, but concentrations of solvents may exceed drinking-water standards, especially in some areas with historical and high-intensity urban development.

Additional sources of surface- and groundwater-quality data can be found in USGS Water Resources Inventory of Connecticut —Farmington River Basin (Part 9) (Handman and others, 1986), Upper Housatonic River Basin (Part 6) (Cervione and others, 1972), and Lower Housatonic River Basin (Part 5) (Wilson and others, 1974). These reports are designed to be useful to planners, public officials, water-utility personnel, and others concerned with the development, management, use, conservation, and protection of water resources.

## 1.6. Watershed Budget

### Model Input Data and Methods of Analysis

Key features of understanding and protecting the Highlands water-supply infrastructure include developing detailed water budgets that include precipitation, evaporation rates, and discharge rates of streams, and evaluating factors such as climate, geology, vegetation, and soils that affect the exchange between surface and ground water. A generalized water-budget watershed model, PRMS—Precipitation-Runoff Modeling System—was used to quantify the components of the water budget and to investigate potential changes to the water budget caused by various build-out scenarios. Documentation for the modeling system is available in the PRMS user's manual (Leavesley and others, 1983). In general, PRMS simulates runoff from a basin. Runoff processes include overland flow, groundwater flow, and shallow subsurface flow. Total streamflow comprises the three components of the runoff process. Input to the Highlands PRMS model includes climatic data and parameters describing the physical characteristics of the basin including slope, aspect, elevation, and soil types. Daily total precipitation and maximum and minimum air-temperature data were obtained from a Northeast Regional Climate Center, National Oceanic Atmospheric Administration (NOAA) (written commun., K. Eggleston, 2008). The location names, identification number, latitude and longitude, and elevations of the data stations used in the study are shown in table 4. The climate stations covered the time period from October 1, 1960 to September 30, 2006.

**Table 4.** Climate stations used in the Highlands Precipitation-Runoff Modeling System (PRMS) model.

[NWS, National Weather Service; AP, Airport]

| NWS number | Name | Latitude | Longitude | Elevation (feet) |
|---|---|---|---|---|
| 060227 | BAKERSVILLE | 41.84 | -73.01 | 686 |
| 060299 | BARKHAMSTED | 41.92 | -72.96 | 705 |
| 060973 | BURLINGTON | 41.80 | -72.93 | 510 |
| 061762 | DANBURY | 41.40 | -73.42 | 405 |
| 062658 | FALLS VILLAGE | 41.95 | -73.37 | 550 |
| 063456 | HARTFORD BRADLEY INTL AP | 41.94 | -72.68 | 160 |
| 065445 | NORFOLK 2 SW | 41.97 | -73.22 | 1,340 |
| 069775 | WOODBURY | 41.55 | -73.23 | 650 |
| 190120 | AMHERST | 42.38 | -72.53 | 150 |
| 191821 | DALTON | 42.47 | -73.15 | 1,212 |
| 194131 | LENOX DALE | 42.34 | -73.25 | 1,004 |
| 196414 | PITTSFIELD MUNI AP | 42.43 | -73.29 | 1,194 |
| 199196 | WESTFIELD BARNES MUNI AP | 42.16 | -72.72 | 271 |
| 199371 | WEST OTIS | 42.18 | -73.22 | 1,295 |
| 301761 | COPAKE | 42.11 | -73.55 | 550 |
| 302286 | EAST CHATHAM | 42.44 | -73.50 | 924 |
| 307035 | RHINEBECK 4 SE | 41.88 | -73.87 | 301 |
| 308304 | STORMVILLE | 41.53 | -73.73 | 915 |

The data layers describing the topography, soils, geology, land cover, and forest cover of the Highland basins were assembled using a geographic information system (GIS). Topographic characteristics such as slope and aspect were derived from the National Elevation Dataset (NED) (U.S. Geological Survey, 2001a). The digital elevation dataset has a spatial resolution of approximately 30 meters. Soil characteristics were derived from the State Soil Geographic

(STATSGO) dataset (Natural Resources Conservation Service, 1994). Geologic characteristics were derived from a 1:1,000,000 scale USGS Surficial Materials Map (Soller, 1998). Land-cover characteristics such as impervious cover, land cover, and forest density (canopy cover) were derived from the National Land Cover Dataset (NLCD) 2001 database (U.S. Geological Survey, 2001b). The NLCD has a spatial resolution of 30 meters. The PRMS model uses 43 parameters to characterize the land-surface conditions and processes. Many of the values for these parameters were computed directly from the GIS data layers. Values for other parameters were determined by associating the GIS data layers for each subwatershed to separate matrix tables for geology, soils, and land use (Leavesley and others, 1983).

Output from the PRMS model is a time-series graph of the rate of runoff from the basin (for the period Oct. 1, 1960 through Sep. 30, 2006) and represents the hydrologic response of the basin to precipitation input on the basis of the basin's climatic, hydrologic, and physical characteristics. The simulated daily time-series data from 1960 to 2006 were used to estimate the water budget (average annual total streamflow, runoff, and base flow), herein referred to as "current conditions."

The PRMS model also was used to simulate changes to the water budgets under the current conditions on the basis of two build-out scenarios referred to as high-constraint and low-constraint build-out. The two build-outs are based on current zoning and regulatory constraints that exclude certain land from development. Low-constraint build-out is less restrictive on building than the high-constraint build-out. The low-constraint and high-constraint build-out analyses are described in Section 2-3 Potential Changes and Resources at Risk, Future Change Scenarios—Build out Analysis and Econometric Modeling of the CT/PA Highlands Summary Report (Connecticut–Pennsylvania Highlands Regional Study, written commun., E.A. Ahearn, 2008). A second objective in the development of the PRMS model was to define the groundwater volume for current conditions and determine potential changes in groundwater volume based on two future population scenarios.

The Highlands study area was subdivided into watersheds on the basis of Hydrologic Unit Codes (HUCs). The HUCs refer to a numbering system used to identify the boundaries and the geographic area of drainage basins for the purpose of water-data management. The largest size drainage area is the HUC 8 (identified by an 8-digit number), which corresponds to the entire surface-water drainage area for major river basins such as the Housatonic and Farmington. These large drainage basins have been further subdivided into 17 HUC 10 subwatersheds (identified by a 10-digit number) and 64 HUC 12 subwatersheds (identified by a 12-digit number) that drain specific reaches of streams and tributaries within the larger basin (figs. 8 and 9). The HUC 10 subwatersheds have an average area of approximately 130 $mi^2$ and a maximum area of 284 $mi^2$ (table 5). In contrast, the HUC 12 subwatersheds have an average area of about 30 $mi^2$ and a maximum area of 62 $mi^2$ (table 6). Ten of the 64 HUC 12 subwatersheds are subdivided at stream-gaging stations that are PRMS-mode-verification locations. Water budgets were analyzed at HUC 10 and HUC 12 scales. The HUC 12 subwatersheds are nested within the HUC 10 subwatersheds. The watershed response at the HUC 10 scale is the areally weighted sum of the responses of all HUC 12 subwatersheds within the HUC 10 watersheds. In the PRMS model, the subwatersheds are represented by 74 hydrologic response units (HRU) through which the physical properties affecting streamflow within the HRU are quantified. For this model, the 64 HUC 12 subwatersheds including the 10 subdivided HUC 12 model-verification subwatersheds are used to define 74 HRUs. HUCs were included in the model even when only a small portion of the HUC is in the defined Highlands region.

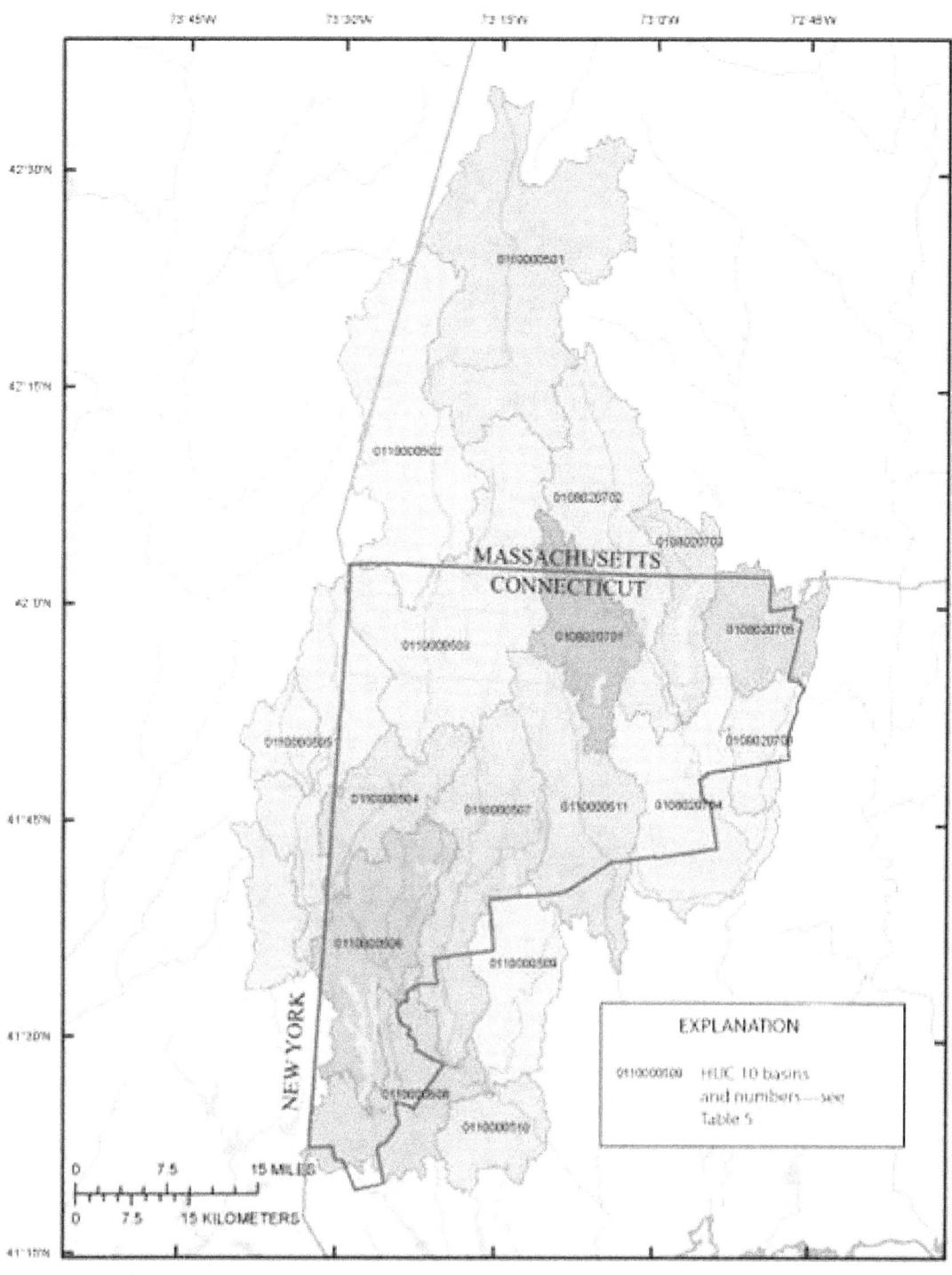

**Figure 8.** Boundaries of the HUC 10 watersheds in the Highlands watershed model.

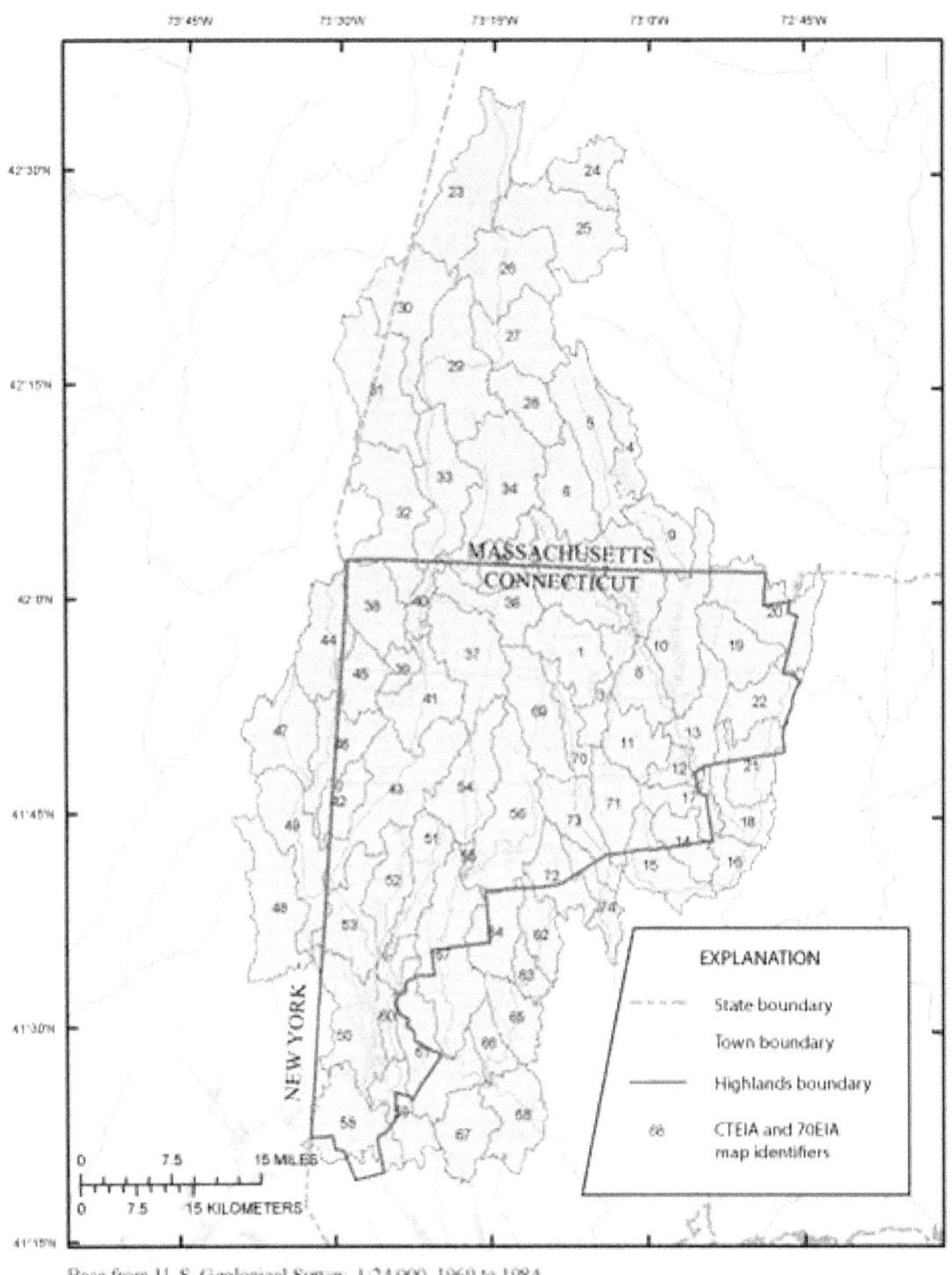

Base from U. S. Geological Survey, 1:24,000, 1969 to 1984
Connecticut State Plane projection
Map identifiers described in CT_HUC12_waterbudget_CTEIA.XLS and
CTEIA_70EIA.XLS

**Figure 9.**     Boundaries of HUC 12 subwatersheds in the Highlands watershed model.

**Table 5.** Description of HUC 10 subwatersheds in the Highlands study area.

[HUC, Hydrologic unit code; mi$^2$, square miles]

| HUC 10 | Drainage area (mi$^2$) | HUC 12 rivers nested within HUC 10 subwatersheds |
|---|---|---|
| 0108020701 | 87.0 | Mad River, Sandy Brook, Still River mainstem |
| 0108020702 | 150 | Otis Reservoir, Clam River, W. Branch Farmington River-headwaters to Clam River and to mouth |
| 0108020703 | 66.0 | Hubbard River, E. Branch Farmington mainstem |
| 0108020704 | 153 | Nepaug River, Farmington River-headwaters to Burlington, Mine Brook, Pequabuck River, Farmington River-Burlington Brook to Thompson Brook |
| 0108020705 | 72.3 | W. Branch Salmon Brook, Salmon Brook |
| 0108020706 | 48.2 | Farmington River - Thompson Brook to Hop Brook and Hop Brook to mouth |
| 0110000501 | 284 | W. Branch Housatonic River, Wahconah Falls Brook, E. Branch Housatonic River, Housatonic River-East Branch to Washington Mountain Brook, Housatonic River-Washington Mountain Brook to Hop Brook, Hop Brook, Housatonic River-Hop Brook to Williams River |
| 0110000502 | 190 | Williams River, Green River, Hubbard Brook, Housatonic mainstem-Williams River to Konkapot River |
| 0110000503 | 231 | Konkapot River, Whiting River, Blackberry River, Hollenbeck River, Salmon Creek, Housatonic mainstem-Konkapot River to Furnace Brook |
| 0110000504 | 79.5 | Macedonia Brook, Housatonic mainstem-Furnace Brook to Tenmile River |
| 0110000505 | 211 | Webatuck Creek-headwaters to Wassaic River, Mudge Pond Brook, Webatuck Creek, Wassaic Creek, Swamp River, Tenmile mainstem |
| 0110000506 | 131 | Candlewood Lake, East and West Aspetuck River, Housatonic mainstem-Tenmile river to Still River |
| 0110000507 | 155 | Shepaug River, Bantam River |
| 0110000508 | 117 | Still River, Housatonic mainstem-Still River to Pootatuck River |
| 0110000509 | 89.0 | Nonnewaug River, Weekeepeemee River, Pomperaug River |
| 0110000510 | 57.4 | Pootatuck River, Housatonic mainstem-Pootatuck River to Naugatuck River |
| 0110000511 | 140 | W. Branch and E. Branch Naugatuck River, Leadmine Brook, Branch Brook, Naugatuck mainstem-E. Branch to Hancock Brook |

**Table 6.**  Description of HUC 12 subwatersheds in the Highlands study area.

[mi$^2$, square miles]

| Map ID (from fig. 9) | HUC 12 | Drainage area (mi$^2$) | HUC 12 river name |
|---|---|---|---|
| 1 | 010802070101 | 31.7 | Mad River |
| 2 | 010802070102 | 37.4 | Sandy Brook |
| 3 | 010802070103 | 17.9 | Still River mainstem |
| 4 | 010802070201 | 15.8 | Otis Reservoir |
| 5 | 010802070202 | 43.7 | West Branch Farmington River-headwaters to Clam River |
| 6 | 010802070203 | 31.4 | Clam River |
| 7 | 010802070204 | 37.8 | West Branch Farmington River-Clam River to mouth |
| 8 | 010802070204 | 21.0 | West Branch Farmington River-Clam River to mouth |
| 9 | 010802070301 | 20.9 | Hubbard River |
| 10 | 010802070302 | 45.2 | East Branch Farmington mainstem |
| 11 | 010802070401 | 23.8 | Nepaug River |
| 12 | 010802070401 | 8.2 | Nepaug River |
| 13 | 010802070402 | 25.9 | Farmington River-headwaters to Burlington Brook |
| 14 | 010802070403 | 18.6 | Mine Brook |
| 15 | 010802070404 | 27.0 | Pequabuck River |
| 16 | 010802070404 | 12.1 | Pequabuck River |
| 17 | 010802070405 | 16.9 | Farmington River-Burlington Brook to Thompson Brook |
| 18 | 010802070405 | 20.3 | Farmington River-Burlington Brook to Thompson Brook |
| 19 | 010802070501 | 26.6 | West Branch Salmon Brook |
| 20 | 010802070502 | 45.7 | Salmon Brook |
| 21 | 010802070601 | 25.0 | Farmington River-Thompson Brook to Hop Brook |
| 22 | 010802070602 | 23.1 | Farmington River-Hop Brook to mouth |
| 23 | 011000050101 | 60.3 | West Branch Housatonic River |
| 24 | 011000050102 | 21.5 | Wahconah Falls Brook |
| 25 | 011000050103 | 49.4 | East Branch Housatonic River |
| 26 | 011000050104 | 40.9 | Housatonic River-East Branch to Washington Mountain Brook |
| 27 | 011000050105 | 36.3 | Housatonic River-Washington Mountain Brook to Hop Brook |
| 28 | 011000050106 | 22.2 | Hop Brook |
| 29 | 011000050107 | 53.0 | Housatonic River-Hop Brook to Williams River |
| 30 | 011000050201 | 44.2 | Williams River |
| 31 | 011000050202 | 53.3 | Green River |
| 32 | 011000050203 | 50.1 | Hubbard Brook |
| 33 | 011000050204 | 42.8 | Housatonic mainstem-Williams River to Konkapot River |
| 34 | 011000050301 | 61.7 | Konkapot River |
| 35 | 011000050302 | 18.9 | Whiting River |
| 36 | 011000050303 | 27.1 | Blackberry River |
| 37 | 011000050304 | 42.9 | Hollenbeck River |
| 38 | 011000050305 | 29.4 | Salmon Creek |
| 39 | 011000050305 | 8.6 | Salmon Creek |
| 40 | 011000050306 | 9.6 | Housatonic mainstem-Konkapot River to Furnace Brook |
| 41 | 011000050306 | 32.9 | Housatonic mainstem-Konkapot River to Furnace Brook |
| 42 | 011000050401 | 17.5 | Macedonia Brook |
| 43 | 011000050402 | 62.0 | Housatonic mainstem-Furnace Brook to Tenmile River |

**Table 6.** Description of HUC 12 subwatersheds in the Highlands study area.—Continued

| | HUC 12 | Drainage area (mi$^2$) | HUC 12 river name |
|---|---|---|---|
| 44 | 011000050501 | 34.4 | Webatuck Creek-headwaters to Wassaic Creek |
| 45 | 011000050502 | 18.9 | Mudge Pond Brook |
| 46 | 011000050503 | 30.3 | Webatuck Creek |
| 47 | 011000050504 | 37.4 | Wassaic Creek |
| 48 | 011000050505 | 47.5 | Swamp River |
| 49 | 011000050506 | 42.2 | Tenmile mainstem |
| 50 | 011000050601 | 40.5 | Candlewood Lake |
| 51 | 011000050602 | 25.3 | East Aspetuck River |
| 52 | 011000050603 | 25.5 | West Aspetuck River |
| 53 | 011000050604 | 40.1 | Housatonic mainstem-Tenmile River to Still River |
| 54 | 011000050701 | 38.4 | Shepaug River-headwaters to Bantam River |
| 55 | 011000050701 | 2.2 | Shepaug River-headwaters to Bantam River |
| 56 | 011000050702 | 54.8 | Bantam River |
| 57 | 011000050703 | 60.0 | Shepaug River-Bantam River to mouth |
| 58 | 011000050801 | 39.6 | Still River-headwaters to Limekiln Brook |
| 59 | 011000050802 | 22.8 | Still River-Limekiln Brook to mouth |
| 60 | 011000050802 | 9.0 | Still River-Limekiln Brook to mouth |
| 61 | 011000050803 | 45.7 | Housatonic mainstem-Still River to Pootatuck River |
| 62 | 011000050901 | 17.7 | Nonewaug River |
| 63 | 011000050901 | 9.4 | Nonewaug River |
| 64 | 011000050902 | 27.1 | Weekeepeemee River |
| 65 | 011000050903 | 21.1 | Pomperaug River |
| 66 | 011000050903 | 13.7 | Pomperaug River |
| 67 | 011000051001 | 26.1 | Pootatuck River |
| 68 | 011000051003 | 31.2 | Housatonic mainstem-Pootatuck River to Naugatuck River |
| 69 | 011000051101 | 34.0 | West Branch Naugatuck River |
| 70 | 011000051102 | 14.1 | East Branch Naugatuck River |
| 71 | 011000051103 | 24.7 | Leadmine Brook |
| 72 | 011000051104 | 22.6 | Branch Brook |
| 73 | 011000051105 | 27.8 | Naugatuck mainstem-East Branch to Hancock Brook |
| 74 | 011000051105 | 17.0 | Naugatuck mainstem-East Branch to Hancock Brook |

The PRMS model simulations are based on the following assumptions: 1) precipitation does not vary from existing conditions to future build-out scenarios; 2) future domestic water-supply needs are met from ground water; 3) water withdrawn from domestic wells is returned near the point of withdrawal by a septic system; and 4) not all the impervious area within a watershed is effective; some portions function as pervious. The effective impervious area (EIA) of a basin is an important parameter in the rainfall to runoff process because it directly affects the volume of runoff and the amount of infiltration recharging water-bearing aquifers. Impervious surfaces such as rooftops, asphalt, and concrete prevent the infiltration of water into the ground. However, these surfaces commonly drain to other areas where the water can infiltrate. Hydrologic modeling of watersheds in the New York–New Jersey and Pennsylvania Highlands Regional Studies assumed 70 percent of the total impervious area is effectively acting as impervious area (Hoppe, 2003).

Recent watershed modeling of the Pomperaug River Basin in western Connecticut included an equation to improve the overall accuracy of the EIA (Appendix 2). In the current study, three additional PRMS model simulations were performed using the Pomperaug EIA equation, herein referred to as CT EIA, from the Pomperaug River watershed model. The three additional model simulations using the CT EIA equation include current conditions, low-constraint build-out analysis, and high-constraint build-out analysis.

## Water-Budget Estimates

Estimates of the water-budget components derived from the PRMS model—evapotranspiration, total streamflow, runoff, and base flow—are summarized in Appendix 1, CT_HUC10_70EIA and CT_HUC12_70EIA provide the 70 percent EIA data for the HUC 10 and HUC 12 subwatersheds, respectively; Appendix 1, CT_HUC10_CTEIA and CT_HUC12_CTEIA provide the data from the CT EIA equation for the HUC 10 and HUC 12 subwatersheds, respectively. The effects of water-budget changes can be evaluated by comparing the model-simulation results for the current conditions (average annual for the period 1960-2006) with simulation results from (1) the low-constraint build-out scenario, and (2) the high-constraint build-out scenario across the HUC 10 and HUC 12 subwatersheds.

The following data are provided for each HUC 10 and HUC 12 subwatershed:
☐ Map ID ( fig. 9, HUC 12 only)
☐ Watershed/subwatershed name (based on stream name or stream segment draining the basin)
☐ Area, in square miles
☐ Hydrologic unit codes (HUC 8, HUC 10, AND HUC 12 digits)
☐ Average annual precipitation, in inches per year

For the current conditions, high-constraint scenario, and low-constraint scenario model simulations, the following information is provided for each subwatershed:
☐ Evapotranspiration, in inches per year
☐ Total streamflow, in inches per year
☐ Runoff, in inches per year
☐ Base flow, in inches per year
☐ Percent total impervious area
☐ Percent effective impervious area
☐ Groundwater withdrawals from domestic wells, in inches per year

These data were specifically used to develop the regional water budget for the Highlands (fig. 10) and determine the percentage of total streamflow that is base flow (fig. 11). The PRMS model divides the flow regime into three components: surface runoff, subsurface flow, and ground water. Base flow is considered to be the groundwater component of the flow regime plus a portion of the subsurface flow. Model results indicate that, on average, base flow made up approximately 65 percent of total streamflow over the Highlands region (74 HUC 12 subwatersheds) from October 1960 to September 2006. The percentage of base flow ranged from 23 to 86 for individual subwatersheds, and the range of base-flow contribution for the individual subwatersheds was 1.2 to 62 Mgal/d, depending in large part on the watershed area.

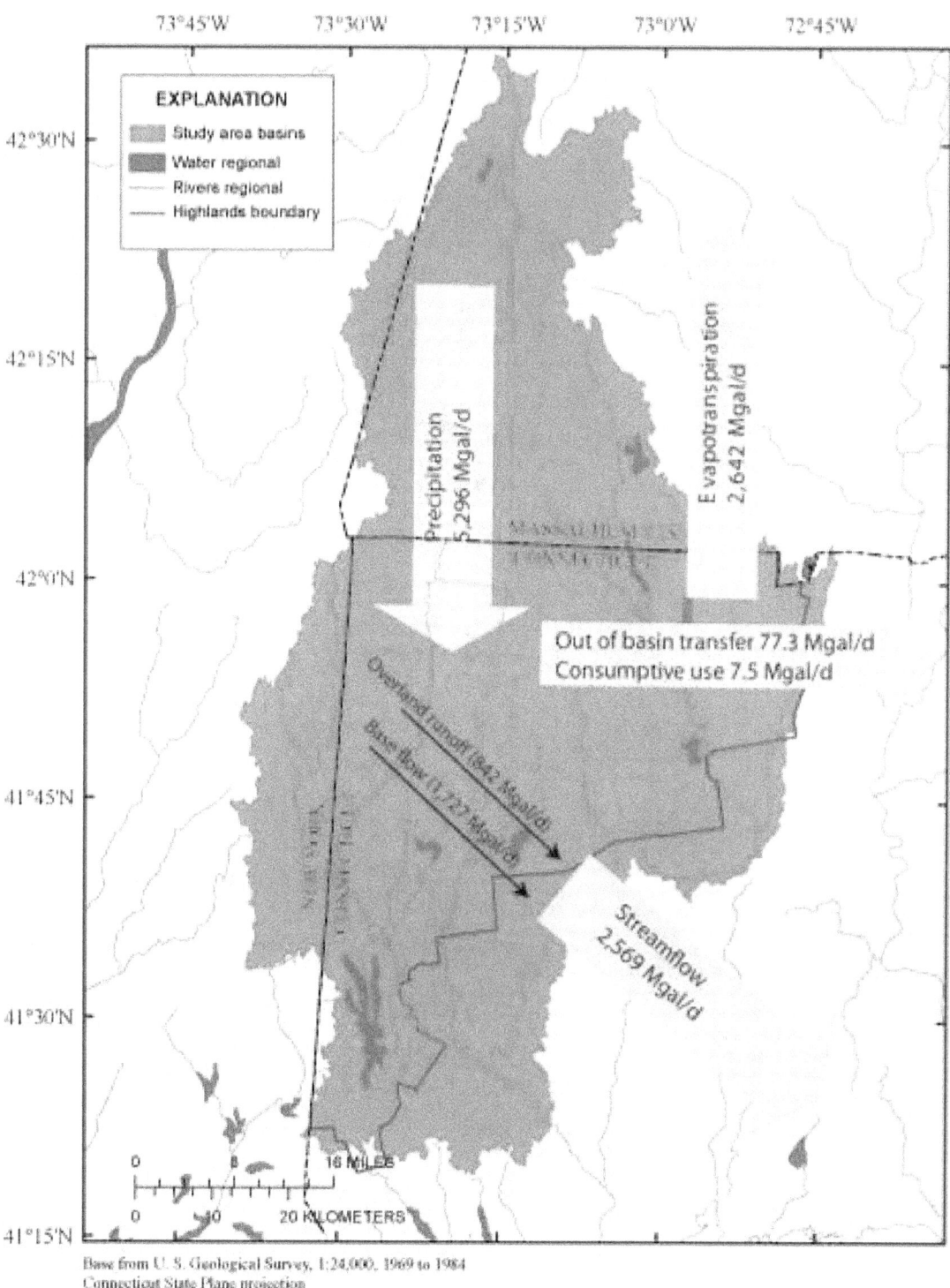

**Figure 10.** Regional water budget for the Highlands, 2006. On an average annual basis, the Highlands receive about 49 inches of precipitation, which is the equivalent of 5,296 Mgal/d. Water that leaves the Highlands includes evapotranspiration (2,642 Mgal/d), streamflow (2,569 Mgal/d), transfers (77.3 Mgal/d), and consumptive use (7.5 Mgal/d).

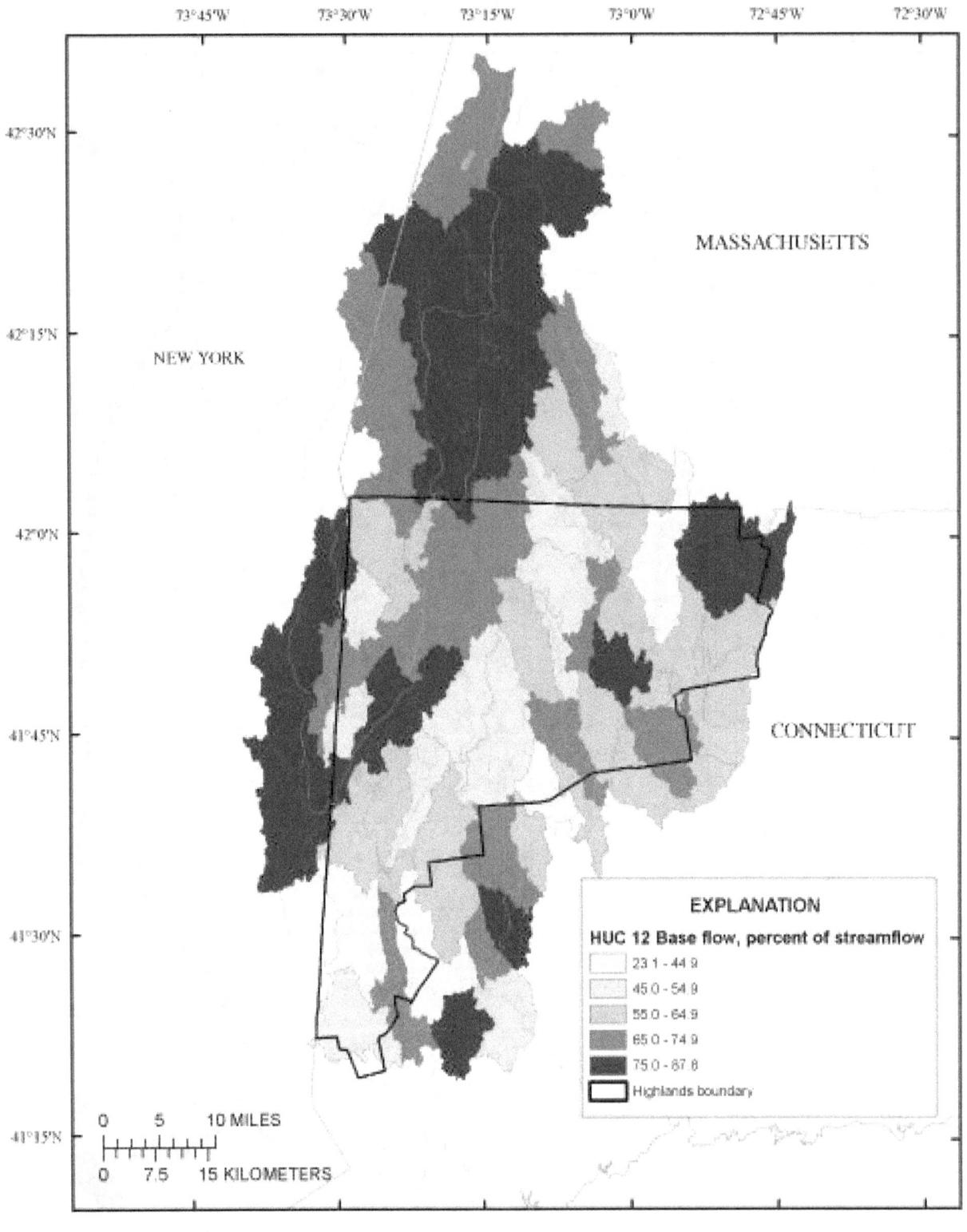

**Figure 11.** Variations in base flow by subwatersheds. The percentage of total streamflow that is base flow was calculated from model-generated water budgets for each HUC 12 subwatershed using the 1960-2006 average climate and impervious-surface data.

## Changes in Water-Budget Estimates for High- and Low-Constraint Build-Out Scenarios

Information from the two build-out analyses (low-constraint and high-constraint) conducted by the Regional Plan Association (J. Cox, Regional Plan Association, written commun., 2008) was incorporated into the PRMS model to simulate the effects of increased impervious area and increased groundwater withdrawals on the various water-budget components—streamflow, runoff, base flow, and evapotranspiration. The low-constraint scenario represents a greater increase in impervious area and consequently a larger impact on the water budget than the high-constraint scenario. Using impervious-surface information derived from the low-constraint build-out scenario, the simulated total impervious area increased from 2.6 to 6.7 percent. For current land-cover conditions, five subwatersheds have greater than 10 percent total impervious area. For the low-constraint build-out, 13 subwatersheds have greater than 10 percent total impervious area. The maximum increase in total impervious area for the low-constraint build-out condition for any HUC 12 subwatershed is 8.9 percent; about 40 percent (22 of 53) of the subwatersheds had a greater than 5-percent increase. For the high-constraint build-out, eight subwatersheds have greater than 10 percent total impervious area. The maximum increase in total impervious area for the high-constraint build-out condition for any HUC 12 subwatershed is 6.8 percent; about 20 percent (11 of 53) of the subwatersheds had a greater than 5-percent increase. The percent increase in total impervious area is based on impervious areas for 53 subwatersheds that lie within the Highlands boundary.

As the percentage of impervious area in a subwatershed increases, runoff increases, base flow decreases, and total streamflow increases. In general, as impervious area increases, runoff increases more than base flow decreases because of a reduction in evapotranspiration. The change in runoff, base flow, and total streamflow resulting from increasing amounts of change in the effective impervious area in the model HUC 12 subwatersheds is shown in figure 12. The linear relations imply changes in the water-budget components are directly proportional to the changes in the effective impervious surface up to the maximum change simulated, which is approximately 6 percent.

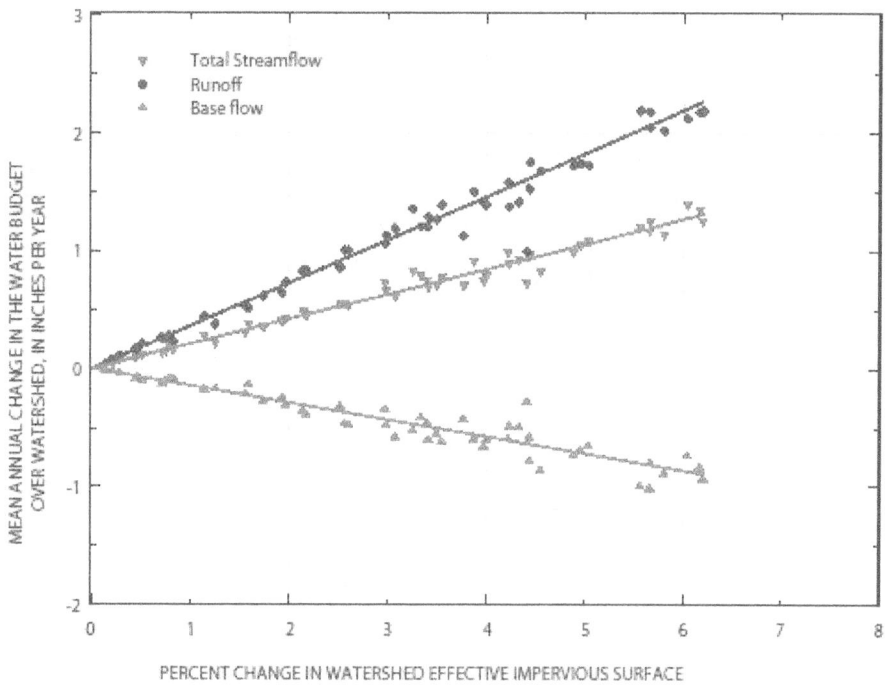

**Figure 12.** Changes in water-budget components in relation to percent change in effective impervious surface as modeled for the Highlands.

31

Research from the University of Connecticut Cooperative Extension System suggests that where greater than 10 percent of a watershed is covered with impervious area, streams are likely impacted and overall water quality is degraded (University of Connecticut, 1994). The effects from the distribution of the impervious area within a watershed have not been fully evaluated.

Under the high-constraint and low-constraint build-out scenarios, the population was estimated to be 560,000 and 670,000 people, respectively. The projected groundwater withdrawals for the two build-out scenarios were calculated by multiplying the population by an average rate of water use of 85 gal/d per person. Under the low-constraint scenario, groundwater withdrawals increased from 11.7 to about 44 Mgal/d (new withdrawals of 32 Mgal/d) from current conditions assuming a population increase of 370,000 people. Under the high-constraint scenario, groundwater withdrawals increased from 11.7 to about 34 Mgal/d (new withdrawals of 22 Mgal/d) from current conditions assuming a population increase of 270,000 people. Groundwater withdrawals were based on population increases for the 28 towns and cities within the Highlands boundary and were not estimated for upstream subwatersheds in Massachusetts. Groundwater withdrawals were not subtracted from the base flows in the water budget because it was assumed that water withdrawn from domestic wells would be returned to the ground water by a nearby septic system. The impervious areas (in percent) and the groundwater withdrawals (in inches per year) for the subwatersheds for the current conditions, high- and low-constraint build-out analysis of the Highlands study area are shown in figure 13 and figure 14, respectively. The water-budget changes simulated from the PRMS model show increases in runoff (fig. 15) and total streamflow (fig. 16) and decreases in base flows (fig. 17). For the low-constraint build-out scenario based on the 70-percent EIA methodology, runoff increased by 76 Mgal/d, total streamflow increased by 45 Mgal/d, and base flow decreased by 31 Mgal/d. For the high-constraint build-out, runoff increased by 55 Mgal/d, total streamflow increased by 32 Mgal/d, and base flow decreased by 23 Mgal/d. The predicted change in runoff and base flow at the HUC 12 watershed scale under the low-constraint development scenario is shown in figure 18. The areas of moderate and greatest change are directly related to the projected increase in impervious-surface area and groundwater withdrawals. The predicted change is expressed as the sum of the absolute values of the runoff and base flow.

Additional model simulations based on the CT EIA equation for the two build-out scenarios (high- and low-constraint) yielded smaller changes to the water budget than the model simulations based on the 70-percent EIA methodology. For the low-constraint scenario, runoff increased by 21 Mgal/d; total streamflow increased by 12 Mgal/d; and base flow decreased by 8 Mgal/d. For the high-constraint build-out scenario, runoff increased by 16 Mgal/d; total streamflow increased by 9 Mgal/d; and base flow decreased by 6 Mgal/d. The results from the PRMS model simulations based on the EIA methodology in the New York-New Jersey Highlands study and the CT EIA equation provide an upper and lower range of potential changes to the water budgets. For example, increases in runoff ranged from 21 to 76 Mgal/d; increases in total streamflow ranged from 12 to 45 Mgal/d; and decreases in base flow ranged from 8 to 31 Mgal/d for the low-constraint build-out scenario based on the CT EIA equation and 70-percent EIA, respectively.

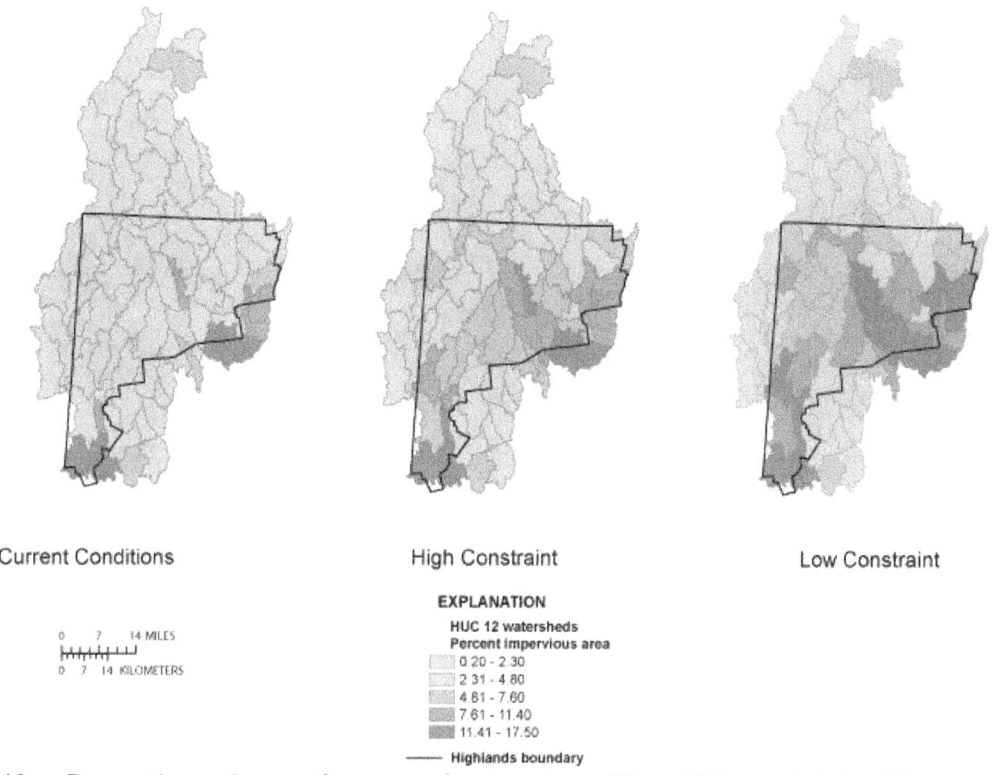

**Figure 13.** Percent impervious surface cover for current conditions, high-constraint and low-constraint build-out scenarios used in the Precipitation Runoff Modeling System (PRMS) of the Highlands study area.

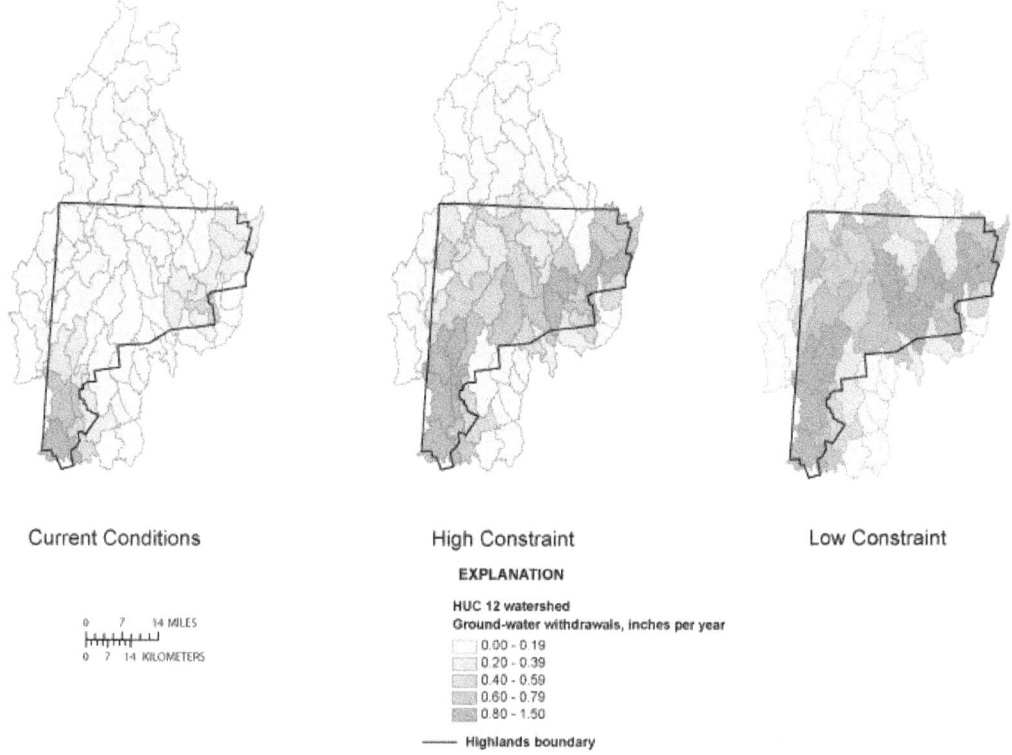

**Figure 14.** Groundwater withdrawals for current conditions, high-constraint and low-constraint build-out scenarios of the Highlands study area

33

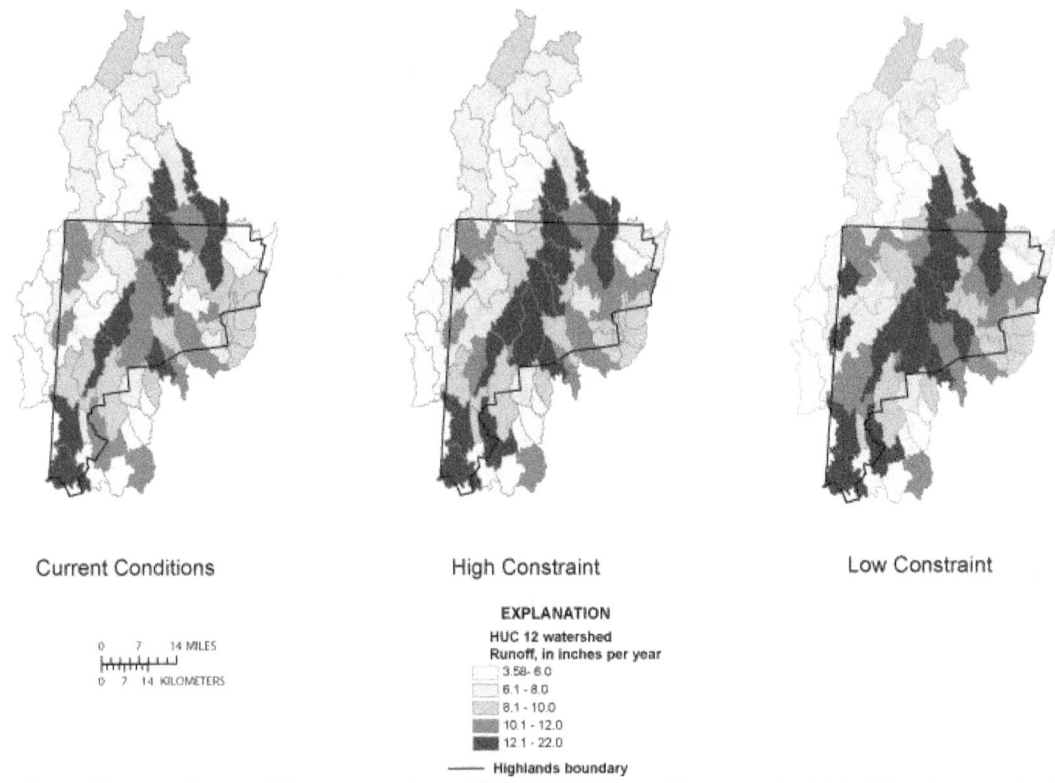

**Figure 15.** Changes in runoff from current conditions to high- and low-constraint build-out scenarios in the Highlands study area using the 70-percent effective impervious area.

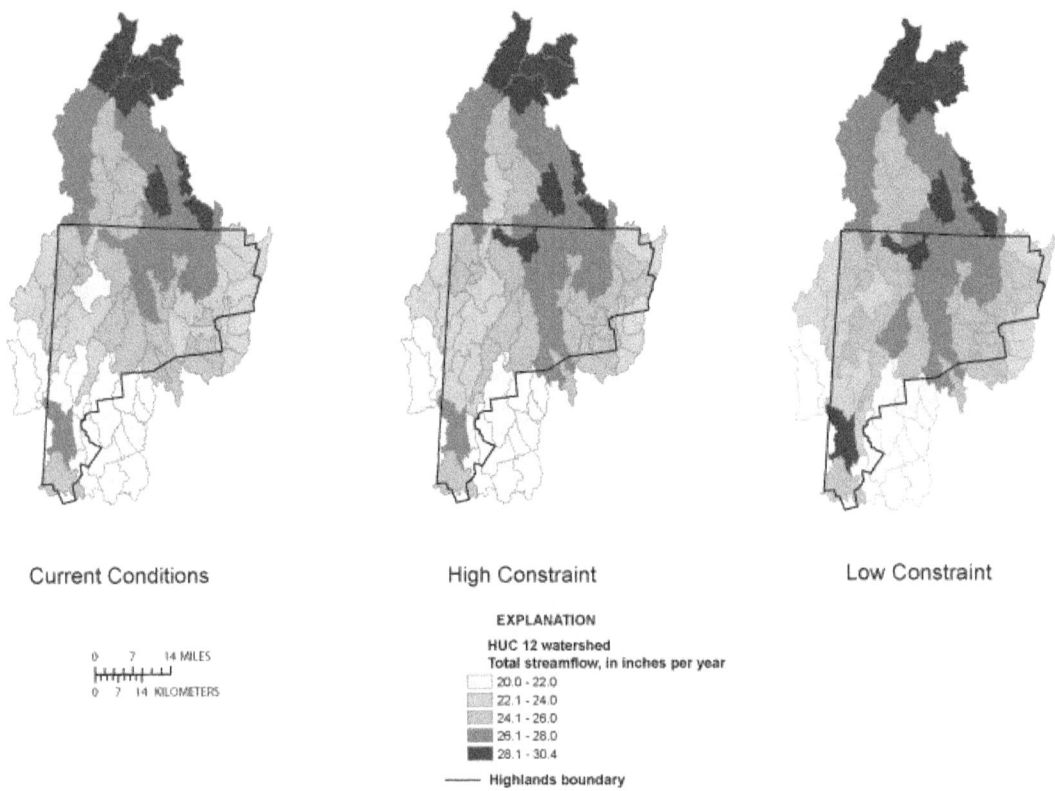

**Figure 16.** Changes in total streamflow from current conditions to high- and low-constraint build-out scenarios in the Highlands study area using the 70-percent effective impervious area.

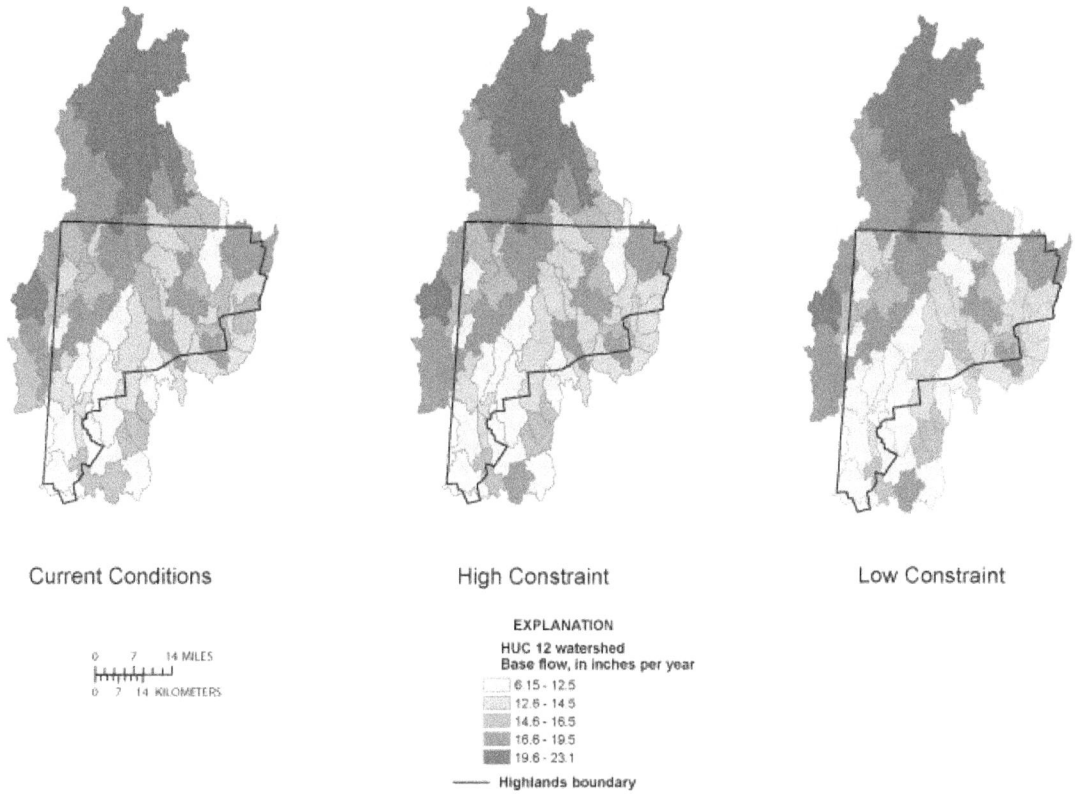

**Figure 17.** Changes in base flow from current conditions to high- and low-constraint build-out scenarios in the Highlands study area using the 70-percent effective impervious area.

Although the water-budget estimates did not account for increases in impervious areas or groundwater withdrawals in the subwatersheds outside Connecticut, the predicted changes—increased runoff, decreased base flow, and an overall increase in streamflow—can be expected in those subwatersheds as well. It is important to note that the quantity and quality of water in the Highlands headwater streams draining from Massachusetts are of considerable importance to water-resources planning and management in the Highlands study area. Additional increases in groundwater withdrawals and impervious areas in the upstream drainage basins would most likely change the water-budget estimates and put additional stresses on the resource by reducing water availability and degrading the water quality of the streams.

## Model Verification and Comparison of Results

Simulation results from the PRMS model were examined graphically and statistically and comparisons of simulated and observed streamflow hydrographs for the gaged watersheds were made. Statistical summaries of the simulated and observed streamflow and base flow for gaged watersheds are shown in table 7.

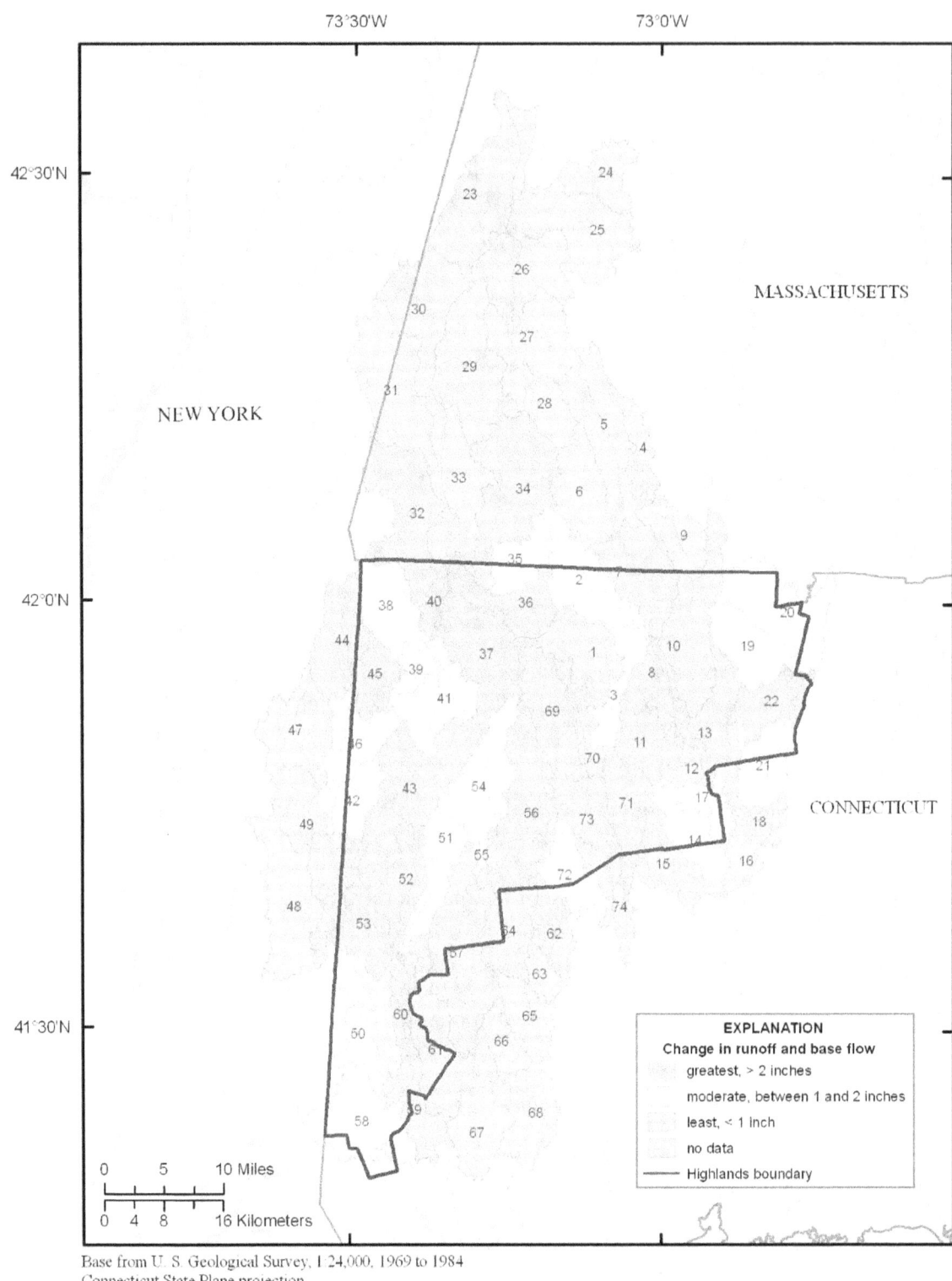

**Figure 18.** Predicted change in runoff and base flow at the HUC 12 watershed scale under the low-constraint development scenario.

**Table 7.** Annual mean flows for U.S. Geological Survey gaging stations compared to annual mean flows simulated from the PRMS model.

[mi², square miles; ft³/s, cubic feet per second; (ft³/s)/mi², cubic feet per second per square mile; unk, unknown; stdev, standard deviation]

| River name | Subwatershed ID (from fig. 18) | Drainage Area (mi²) | Years of Record (water years[1]) | Diversions | Regulation | Annual Mean Streamflow Observed (ft³/s) | Annual Mean Streamflow Simulated from PRMS (ft³/s) | Annual Mean Streamflow Error Fraction Percent | Baseflow Fraction Percent (PART program) | Baseflow Fraction Percent (PRMS model) | Streamflow per unit area Observed ((ft³/s)/mi²) | Streamflow per unit area Simulated from PRMS ((ft³/s)/mi²) |
|---|---|---|---|---|---|---|---|---|---|---|---|---|
| | | | | | | **Least Disturbed** | | | | | | |
| East Branch Salmon Brook | 20 | 39.5 | 1964-1976 | minor | minor | 65 | 64 | -0.02 | 77% | 74% | 1.65 | 1.62 |
| Leadmine Brook | 71 | 19.6 | 1961-1973 | minor | minor | 37 | 30 | -0.19 | 69% | 59% | 1.89 | 1.53 |
| Pomperaug River | 62,63,64,65 | 75.1 | 1961-2006 | minor | minor | 132 | 118 | -0.11 | 70% | 73% | 1.76 | 1.57 |
| Sandy Brook | 2 | 34.9 | 1968-1976 | minor | minor | 83 | 74 | -0.10 | 62% | 50% | 2.37 | 2.13 |
| Tenmile River | 44,45,46,47,48,49 | 203 | 1961-2006 | minor | minor | 318 | 332 | 0.04 | 78% | 78% | 1.57 | 1.64 |
| Nepaug Brook | 11 | 23.5 | 1961-1972 | none | none | 38 | 34 | -0.11 | 66% | 76% | 1.62 | 1.45 |
| West Aspetuck River | 52 | 23.8 | 1963-1972 | minor | minor | 34 | 33 | -0.03 | 77% | 59% | 1.43 | 1.39 |
| Hubbard Brook | 9 | 19.9 | 1961-2006 | none | none | 42 | 44 | 0.05 | 58% | 57% | 2.11 | 2.21 |
| Salmon River | 38 | 29.4 | 1962-2006 | minor | minor | 50 | 55 | 0.10 | 78% | 60% | 1.70 | 1.87 |
| | | | | | | **Most Disturbed** | | | | | | |
| Blackberry River | 35,36 | 45.9 | 1961-1971 | unk | flood | 60 | 70 | 0.17 | 66% | 82% | 1.31 | 1.53 |
| W Br. Farmington River | 4,5,6,7 | 131 | 1961-2006 | supply reservoir supply | reservoir, power plant | 255 | 268 | 0.05 | 77% | 63% | 1.95 | 2.05 |
| W Br Naugatuck River | 69 | 33.8 | 1961-1996 | diversion | flood | 60 | 65 | 0.08 | 64% | 57% | 1.78 | 1.92 |
| E Br. Naugatuck River | 70 | 13.6 | 1961-1996 | unk | flood | 25 | 24 | -0.04 | 69% | 56% | 1.84 | 1.76 |
| Still River | 1,2,3 | 85 | 1961-2006 | unk supply | reservoir, power plant | 171 | 164 | -0.04 | 65% | 54% | 2.01 | 1.93 |
| Mad River | 1 | 18.5 | 1961-1967 | supply | flood | 19 | 26 | 0.38 | 65% | 52% | 1.02 | 1.41 |
| Pequabuck River | 15,16 | 45.8 | 1961-2006 | reservoir supply | reservoir outlet | 82 | 78 | -0.05 | 70% | 67% | 1.80 | 1.70 |
| Shepaug River at Woodville | 54 | 38.1 | 1961-1966,2001, 2006 1961- | supply reservoir upstrea m supply | reservoir outlet upstream reservoir | 46 | 60 | 0.29 | 68% | 46% | 1.21 | 1.56 |
| Shepaug River at Roxbury | 54,55,56,57 | 132 | 1971,2002-2006 | reservoir | reservoir outlet | 212 | 188 | -0.11 | 76% | 55% | 1.60 | 1.42 |
| | | | | | | **Summary Statsitics** | | | | | | |
| | All Rivers | Mean | | | | 96.05 | 95.94 | 0.02 | 70% | 62% | 1.70 | 1.71 |
| | All Rivers | Stdev | | | | 86.76 | 87.52 | 0.14 | 6% | 10% | 0.33 | 0.26 |
| | Least Disturbed Rivers | Mean | | | | 88.73 | 87.17 | -0.04 | 71% | 65% | 1.79 | 1.71 |
| | Least Disturbed Rivers | Stdev | | | | 91.49 | 95.86 | 0.09 | 7% | 10% | 0.29 | 0.29 |
| | Most Disturbed Rivers | Mean | | | | 103.37 | 104.72 | 0.08 | 69% | 59% | 1.61 | 1.70 |
| | Most Disturbed Rivers | Stdev | | | | 86.64 | 83.15 | 0.17 | 5% | 10% | 0.35 | 0.23 |

[1] A water year is the 12-month period October 1 through September 30. The water year is designated by the calendar year in which it ends.

Annual mean streamflow and annual mean base-flow estimates simulated from the PRMS model were compared to statistical analysis and streamflow partitioning of streamflow data from USGS gages with at least 5 years of continuous-flow record within the Highlands study area. Both relatively natural rivers and disturbed rivers were compared (streamflow is considered artificially increased or decreased by water withdrawals, out-of-basin transfers, point-source discharges, regulation, and (or) reservoir operations).

Overall, the estimates of annual mean streamflow simulated from the PRMS model are within 2 percent of the observed annual mean streamflow from USGS gaging stations. For rivers with disturbed flow conditions, PRMS overestimated the annual mean streamflow by an average of 8 percent, which may be an indication of the out-of-basin diversions not accounted for in the model. For the rivers with natural-flow conditions, PRMS underestimated the annual mean streamflow by an average of 4 percent, indicating that the model slightly under predicts annual mean streamflow.

The base-flow fraction of total streamflow simulated by the PRMS model was comparable to the base-flow estimates derived from the PART program, which uses streamflow partitioning to estimate base flow from the daily streamflow record (described in section "Base-flow determination at selected gaging stations"). Overall, the estimates from PRMS are slightly lower than the estimates from the PART program. For the rivers with relatively natural rivers flow conditions, the base-flow fraction of total streamflow is 65 and 71 percent from PRMS and PART, respectively. For the disturbed rivers, the base-flow fraction of total streamflow is 59 percent and 69 percent from PRMS and PART, respectively. To some extent, the higher base-flow estimates from the PART program may be explained by regulated releases that artificially increase base flow; the PART program interprets most regulated releases as base flow.

Numerical watershed models simplify the complex processes and physical characteristics of a basin. It should be noted that in this study, the PRMS model of the Connecticut Highlands did not include (1) major groundwater and surface-water withdrawals from municipal water supply and commercial/industrial uses, (2) wastewater-return flows, (3) out-of-basin flows, (4) in-stream flow releases from reservoirs, and (4) groundwater withdrawals from private wells. Subsequently, the PRMS model parameters and coefficient values for the gaged watersheds were not calibrated to closely simulate runoff, streamflow, and base flow of the gaged watersheds. Model simulation results are subject to various sources of uncertainty. Some uncertainties are inherent in the model structure and some uncertainties are dependent on model development and input data. Consequently, there are uncertainties to the water-budget estimates that should be considered when using its results for water-resources management decisions.

## Selected References

Alley, W.M., and Veenhuis, J.E., 1983, Effective impervious area in urban runoff modeling: Journal of Hydraulic Engineering, v. 109, no. 2, p. 313-319.

Cervione, M.A., Jr., Mazzafero, D.L., and Melvin, R.L., 1972, Water resources inventory of Connecticut; Part 6, Upper Housatonic River basin, Connecticut: Connecticut Water Resources Bulletin 21, 84 p.

Connecticut Department of Environmental Protection, 2008, Lists of registered and permitted diversions: Hartford, Conn., accessed December 29, 2008, at *http://www.ct.gov/dep/cwp/view.asp?a=2720&q=404934&depNav_GID=1654*

Connecticut Department of Public Health, 2008a, Drinking water section: Hartford, Conn., accessed December 29, 2008, at *http://www.ct.gov/dph/cwp/view.asp?a=3139&q=387304&dphNav_GID=1824*

Connecticut Department of Public Health, 2008b, Public water system classifications and inverntory: Hartford, Conn., accessed December 29, 2008, at *http://www.ct.gov/dph/cwp/view.asp?a=3139&q=387346*

Connecticut Department of Public Utility Control, 2008, Water unit: New Britain, Conn., accessed December 29, 2008, at *http://www.ct.gov/dpuc/cwp/view.asp?a=3361&q=415120&dpucNav=|*

Connecticut General Statute 25-32d-4, 2008, *http://www.cga.ct.gov/asp/menu/statutes.asp*

Grady, S.J., and Mullaney, J.R., 1998, Natural and human factors affecting shallow water quality in surficial aquifers in the Connecticut, Housatonic, and Thames River Basins: U.S. Geological Survey Water-Resources Investigations Report 98-4042, 81 p.

Handman, E.H., Haeni, P.F., and Thomas, M.P., 1986, Water resources inventory of Connecticut; Part 9, Farmington River basin, Connecticut: Connecticut Water Resources Bulletin 29, 91 p.

Healy, D.F., 1990, Connecticut water supply and use, with sections on Public-supply water use, by H.D. Sternberg, and Water management, by C.J. Hughes, *in* Carr, J.E., Chase, E.B., Paulson, R.W., and Moody, D.W., comps., National water summary 1987—Hydrologic events and water supply and use: U.S. Geological Survey Water-Supply Paper 2350, p. 193-200.

Hoppe, M.C., compiler, 2003, New York – New Jersey Highlands Regional Study, Technical Report: U.S. Forest Service, NA-TP-04-03, April 2003.

Hoppe, M.C., and Phelps, M.G., 2002, New York – New Jersey Highlands Regional Study, 2002 Update: U.S. Forest Service, NA-TP-02-03, December 2002.

Leavesley, G.H., Lichty, R.W., Troutman, B.M., and Saindon, L.G., 1983, Precipitation-runoff modeling system, user's manual: U.S. Geological Survey Water-Resources Investigations Report 83-4238, 207 p.

Melvin, R.L., Grady, S.J., and Healy, D.F., 1988, Connecticut groundwater quality, with a section on Groundwater quality management, by Fred Banach, *in* Moody, D.W., Carr, Jerry, Chase, E.B., and Paulson, R.W., comps., National water summary 1986—Hydrologic events and groundwater quality: U.S. Geological Survey Water-Supply Paper 2325, p. 191-198.

Miller, D.R., Warner, G.S., Ogden, F.L., and DeGaetano, A.T., 2002, Precipitation in Connecticut: Storrs, Conn., University of Connecticut, Connecticut Institute of Water Resources, 65 p.

Mullaney, J.R., 2004, Water use, groundwater recharge and availability, and quality of water in the Greenwich area, Fairfield County, Connecticut and Westchester County, New York, 2000-2002: U.S. Geological Survey Water-Resources Investigations Report 03-4300, 64 p. Online at http://water.usgs.gov/pubs/wri/wri034300/

Natural Resources Conservation Service, National Soil Survey Center, 1991, STATe Soil GeOgraphic (STATSGO) database: Miscellaneous Publication 1492, 110 p. (revised July, 1994).

University of Connecticut, Cooperative Extension System, NEMO Fact Sheet #3, *"Impacts of Development on Waterways"*; The Center for Watershed Protection's *"Watershed Protection Techniques,"* Vol. 1, No.3, Fall 1994.

Rutledge, A.T., 1993, Computer programs for describing the recession of groundwater discharge and for estimating mean groundwater recharge and discharge from streamflow record: U.S. Geological Survey Water-Resources Investigations Report 93-4121, 45 p.

Rutledge, A.T., 1998, Computer programs for describing the recession of groundwater discharge and for estimating mean groundwater recharge and discharge from streamflow records--Update: U.S. Geological Survey Water-Resources Investigations Report 98-4148, 43 p.

Soller, D.R., and Packard, P.H., 1998, Digital representation of a map showing the thickness and character of quaternary sediments in the glaciated United States east of the Rocky Mountains: U.S. Geological Survey Digital Data Series 38. Online at *http://pubs.usgs.gov/dds/dds38/*.

Solley, W.B., 1998, Estimates of water use in the western United States in 1990, and water-use trends, 1960–90: U.S. Geological Survey Open-File Report 97–176, 15 p.

State of Connecticut, 2008, Source water protection measures: Regulation of Department of Public Health, M-39 Rev. 1/77, accessed December 29, 2008, at *http://www.cwwa.org/pdf/regulation_swp.pdf*

Sutherland, R.C., 2000. Methods for estimating the effective impervious area of urban watersheds, Article 32, *in* Scheler, T.R., and Holland, H.K., eds., The Practice of watershed protection: Ellicott City, Md., Center for Watershed Protection, p.193-195.

University of Connecticut, 1994, Cooperative Extension System, NEMO Fact Sheet #3, "Impacts of Development on Waterways"; The Center for Watershed Protection's "Watershed Protection Techniques," Vol. 1, No.3, Fall 1994.

U.S. Bureau of the Census, 1990, American FactFinder: accessed February 8, 2008, at *http://factfinder.census.gov/servlet/DatasetMainPageServlet?_program=DEC&_tabId=DEC2&_submenuId=datasets_1&_lang=en&_ts=268737827513.*

U.S. Bureau of the Census, 2005, American FactFinder: accessed February 8, 2008, at *http://factfinder.census.gov/servlet/GCTTable?_bm=y&-geo_id=04000US09&-_box_head_nbr=GCT-T1&-ds_name=PEP_2008_EST&-_lang=en&-format=ST-9&-_sse=on*

U.S. Department of Agriculture, Natural Resources Conservation Service, Watershed Boundary Dataset: accessed July 11, 2007 at *http://datagateway.nrcs.usda.gov/*.

U.S. Geological Survey, 1997, STATSGO, Soil characteristics for the conterminous United States: U.S. Geological Survey Open-File Report 656, accessed January 15, 2003, at *http//water.usgs.gov/GIS/metadata/usgswrd/muid.html*

U.S. Geological Survey, 2001a, National elevation dataset: U.S. Geological Survey, accessed October 20, 2003, at *http://gisdata.usgs.gov/NED/*.

U.S. Geological Survey, 2001b, National land cover dataset: U.S. Geological Survey Fact Sheet 108-00, accessed February 18, 2004, at *http://mac.usgs.gov/mac/isb/pubs/factsheets/*.

U.S. Geological Survey, 2008a, USGS groundwater data for Connecticut: National Water Information System—Web interface, accessed December 29, 2008, at http://waterdata.usgs.gov/ct/nwis/gw?

U.S. Geological Survey, 2008b, USGS surface-water data for Connecticut: National Water Information System—Web interface, accessed December 29, 2008, at http://waterdata.usgs.gov/ct/nwis/sw?

U.S. Geological Survey, 2008c, USGS water-quality data for Connecticut: National Water Information System—Web interface, accessed December 29, 2008, at http://waterdata.usgs.gov/ct/nwis/qw?

Wilson, W.E., Burke, E.L., and Thomas, C.E., 1974, Water resources inventory of Connecticut; Part 5, Lower Housatonic River basin, Connecticut: Connecticut Water Resources Bulletin 19, 79 p.

# Appendix 1. Data for Documenting Information Provided in the Connecticut Highlands Technical Report – *Documentation of the Regional Rainfall-Runoff Model*

**(Excel file** CT_Highlands_appendix1.xls **linked to Web page)**

This appendix contains an Excel file with seven worksheets documenting information provided in the Connecticut Highlands Technical Report – *Documentation of the Regional Rainfall-Runoff Model.*

**CT_community_wells** contains estimates of groundwater safe yields for community wells used for municipal supply, industrial, commercial, irrigation, and mining uses.

**CT_streamflow** contains estimates of mean-annual streamflow and mean-annual base flow (groundwater discharge) derived using PART program.

**Domestic_use** contains estimates of domestic water use in the Highlands by Town in 2005.

Estimates of the water-budget components—evapotranspiration, total streamflow, runoff, and base flow—derived from the U.S. Geological Survey Precipitation Runoff Model System (PRMS) are summarized in the following Excel tables: **CT_HUC10_70EIA** and **CT_HUC12_70EIA** provide the data for the HUC 10 and HUC 12 subwatersheds on the basis of the 70 percent EIA, respectively; **CT_HUC10_CTEIA** and **CT_HUC12_CTEIA** provide the data for the HUC 10 and HUC 12 subwatersheds on the basis of the CT EIA equation, respectively.

# Appendix 2. Estimating Effective Impervious Area Using the Connecticut Effective Impervious Area (CT EIA) Equation

The effective impervious area (EIA) is the portion of the total impervious area (TIA) within a basin that includes rooftops, paved driveways, and parking lots connected to storm-sewer systems and results in direct runoff to a stream. Runoff generated on impervious surfaces not directly connected to drainage systems is routed to grassed or wooded areas where some or all of it can infiltrate into the ground. Impervious area that does not contribute directly to runoff is subtracted from the TIA to obtain the EIA.

Empirical equations for determining the EIA have been developed as part of several studies (Alley and Veenhuis, 1983; Sutherland, 2000). In a Connecticut study (D.M. Bjerklie, U.S. Geological Survey, written commun., 2009), the EIA was determined as a function of the TIA computed by an assumed connectedness relation with the following general form (Alley and Veenhuis, 1983):

$$EIA = k_1 * (TIA)^{exp} \tag{1}$$

where,

      EIA    is the effective impervious area, in percent,

      $k_1$    is a constant,

      TIA    is the total impervious area, in percent, and

      exp    is an exponent.

Alley and Veenhuis (1983) assumed the values for $k_1$ and exp are 0.15 and 1.41, respectively, for a "typical" region in the United States with storm sewers in place. The Alley and Veenhuis equation was modified for Connecticut using streamflow and precipitation data for the state. Because the streamflow and precipitation data were analyzed with a model that had a daily time step, the storm-runoff analysis was limited to single-day storms. The analysis assumed that the storm hydrograph rose and fell within a single day and that the runoff from the impervious surfaces entered the stream on the same day. Ice and snow cover or saturated ground also can prevent precipitation from infiltrating the ground. In order to limit the analysis to impervious surfaces, the storm-runoff analysis considered only storms from May through October with precipitation amounts of 0.5 in. or less (Zarriello and Barlow, 2002; Zarriello and Ries, 2000).

The runoff analysis described used 18 watersheds in Connecticut. The selected watersheds represented the range of land use and impervious-area percentages in Connecticut. The area of the watersheds was comparable to, or smaller than, the basins used in the Pomperaug River model, such that relative attenuation due to scale effects is limited. Two years of recent streamflow record were analyzed for each of the basins. Suitable runoff events were isolated from the records and then correlated with precipitation records from nearby National Oceanic Atmospheric Administration weather stations.

The weather stations used for the analysis included 12 with a continuous record of precipitation. From one to three stations were used to represent the precipitation for each of the watersheds, depending on proximity of the stations to the watershed of interest. Where more than one station was used, the values from each station were averaged. Thus, the analysis did not attempt to evaluate the spatial distribution of precipitation as it related to the watersheds of interest. Instead, the large number of events winnowed from the data are assumed to average out the errors associated with the use of potentially non-representative stations.

The results of the Pomperaug River study indicate the percent impervious area for the Connecticut watersheds was low compared to the data from Alley and Veenhuis (1983). This reflects the rural nature of the study basins, such as the Pomperaug River Basin. The EIA estimation model for Connecticut is given as:

$$EIA = 0.00013*(TIA)^3 + 0.005*(TIA)^2 + 0.2287*(TIA) \qquad (2)$$

where,

EIA    is the effective impervious area, in percent, and

TIA    is the total impervious area, in percent.

This equation, referred to as the CT EIA in the Highlands Study, is considered appropriate for rural watersheds in the western region of Connecticut. The CT EIA equation provides estimates of EIA that are very comparable to an equation proposed by Sutherland (2000) for somewhat disconnected basins (where 50 percent of the urban areas are serviced by ditches or swales) with some infiltration measures (swales, permeable payments, and or storm-water detention) over the range of impervious surface percentages in the Pomperaug watershed.

## References

Alley, W.M., and Veenhuis, J.E., 1983, Effective impervious area in urban runoff modeling: Journal of Hydraulic Engineering, v. 109, no. 2, p. 313-319.

Sutherland, R.C., 2000. Methods for estimating the effective impervious area of urban watersheds, Article 32, *in* Scheler, T.R., and Holland, H.K., eds., The Practice of watershed protection: Ellicott City, Md., Center for Watershed Protection, p.193-195.

Zarriello, P. J., and Barlow, L.K., 2002, Measured and simulated runoff to the lower Charles River, Massachusetts, October 1999-September 2000: U.S. Geological Survey Water-Resources Investigation Report 2002-4129, 89 p.

Zarriello, P. J., Ries, K.G., III, 2000, A precipitation-runoff model for analysis of the effects of water withdrawals on streamflow, Ipswich River basin, Massachusetts: U.S. Geological Survey Water-Resources Investigation Report 2000-4029, 99 p.

Prepared by the Pembroke Publishing Service Center.

For more information concerning this report, contact:

Director
U.S. Geological Survey
Connecticut Water Science Center
101 Pitkin Street
East Hartford, CT 06108
dc_ct@usgs.gov

or visit our Web site at:
http://ct.water.usgs.gov

www.ingramcontent.com/pod-product-compliance
Lightning Source LLC
Chambersburg PA
CBHW080345290526
45791CB00009BA/2744